Could a Good God Permit
So Much Suffering?

Could a Good God Permit So Much Suffering?

A Debate

JAMES STERBA
and
RICHARD SWINBURNE

OXFORD
UNIVERSITY PRESS

Great Clarendon Street, Oxford, OX2 6DP,
United Kingdom

Oxford University Press is a department of the University of Oxford.
It furthers the University's objective of excellence in research, scholarship,
and education by publishing worldwide. Oxford is a registered trade mark of
Oxford University Press in the UK and in certain other countries

© James Sterba and Richard Swinburne 2024

The moral rights of the authors have been asserted

All rights reserved. No part of this publication may be reproduced, stored in
a retrieval system, or transmitted, in any form or by any means, without the
prior permission in writing of Oxford University Press, or as expressly permitted
by law, by licence or under terms agreed with the appropriate reprographics
rights organization. Enquiries concerning reproduction outside the scope of the
above should be sent to the Rights Department, Oxford University Press, at the
address above

You must not circulate this work in any other form
and you must impose this same condition on any acquirer

Published in the United States of America by Oxford University Press
198 Madison Avenue, New York, NY 10016, United States of America

British Library Cataloguing in Publication Data

Data available

Library of Congress Control Number: 2023952448

ISBN 978–0–19–284854–3 (hbk.)
ISBN 978–0–19–284855–0 (pbk.)

DOI: 10.1093/oso/9780192848543.001.0001

Printed and bound by
CPI Group (UK) Ltd, Croydon, CR0 4YY

Links to third party websites are provided by Oxford in good faith and
for information only. Oxford disclaims any responsibility for the materials
contained in any third party website referenced in this work.

To Peter Montchiloff, Oxford University Editor from 1993 to 2023

Acknowledgements

We are most grateful to Peter Momtchiloff and to the two anonymous readers who read a draft of this book on behalf of Oxford University Press, and provided helpful comments, of which we have taken account in preparing the final version. We would also like to thank the many people with whom each of us has discussed the topic of our book over the years. Richard Swinburne would also like to thank the editors of *Forum Philosophicum* for permission to include much material from a paper of his, 'A Christian Theodicy' published in *Forum Philosophicum*, 28, no. 1 (2023).

Contents

1. Introduction   1
   James Sterba and Richard Swinburne

2. The World's Evils Are Logically Incompatible with God's Existence   7
   James Sterba

3. The World's Evils Are Logically Compatible with God's Existence   31
   Richard Swinburne

4. Response to Swinburne   67
   James Sterba

5. Response to Sterba's Response   111
   Richard Swinburne

Notes   133
Guide to Further Reading   141
Index   145

1
Introduction

James Sterba and Richard Swinburne

The problem of whether a good God would permit so much suffering has traditionally been called the problem of evil. Evils are bad states of affairs that prima facie (seem initially to be such as) ought to be prevented, and suffering is a major component of those evils. In the classical world, the problem of evil might sometimes have been taken as a challenge to the very existence of God or gods of some sort. For example, Epicurus (341–270 BCE) purportedly argued:

> Is God willing to prevent evil, but not able? Then he is not omnipotent. Is he able, but not willing? Then he is malevolent. Is he both able and willing? Then whence cometh evil? Is he neither able nor willing? Then why call him God?[1]

Even so, Epicurus allowed that gods might still exist, although, he claimed, they had nothing to do with human affairs.

During the Middle Ages, the problem of evil was generally taken to be limited to the challenge of providing some explanation for why an all-good, all-powerful God would permit the evil we find in the world. Hardly any medieval thinker claimed that the evil in the world was incompatible with the very existence of the God of traditional theism.

With the coming of the Enlightenment, however, and especially in the writing of David Hume and Baron d'Holbach, just such an interpretation of the problem of evil began to emerge. Later in the nineteenth century, Charles Darwin was deeply troubled by the problem of evil, particularly with regard to the suffering of animals. Just a few months after publishing *The Origin of Species*, Darwin wrote to Harvard botanist Asa Gray, a staunch believer:

I had no intention to write atheistically. But I own that I cannot see as plainly as others do, and as I should wish to do, evidence of design and beneficence on all sides of us. There seems to be too much misery in the world. I cannot persuade myself that a beneficent and omnipotent God would have designedly created the Ichneumonidae with the express intention of their [larvae] feeding within the bodies of living Caterpillars.[2]

Darwin clearly thought that his theory of evolution made it even more difficult to show that an all-good, all-powerful God was compatible with all the evil in the world.

In the twentieth century, John Mackie restated the problem of evil in its more challenging form as follows:

God is omnipotent; God is wholly good; and yet evil exists. There seems to be some contradiction between these three propositions, so that if any two of them were true the third would be false. But at the same time all three are essential parts of most theological positions: the theologian, it seems, at once must and cannot consistently adhere to all three.[3]

In order to see the force of Mackie's challenge, let us analyse the three propositions, which he claimed to be inconsistent. First, 'God is omnipotent', which means 'able to do anything'. But does that mean that God is supposed to be able to make me younger than my father, or to make a person who is both less than five foot tall and also more than six foot tall? Surely not. The normal theistic view is that God can only do the logically possible. A proposition is logically possible if and only if it does not entail a contradiction. (Subsequently, we will use 'iff' as shorthand for 'if and only if'.) One proposition entails another proposition iff someone who asserts the first proposition is thereby committed to the truth of the second proposition. So 'this is red' entails 'this is coloured'; 'there are three foxes in the wood' entails 'there are more than two foxes in the wood'. A contradiction is a proposition which says that something both is and is not so. Hence 'I exist and also I do not exist' is a contradiction; so too is 'all humans are mortal, and some humans are not mortal'. So in the words of the great philosopher-theologian, St Thomas Aquinas, 'whatever does not involve a contradiction is in that realm of the possible with respect to which God is called omnipotent' (*Summa Theologiae* 1a.25.3). So, God cannot make me both less than five feet tall and more than six feet tall, because that entails that I am both not more than six feet tall, and also more than six feet tall—which is a contradiction. More importantly for our purposes here, God cannot allow us to act freely in a certain regard while at the same time preventing us from acting freely in that same regard. Yet the fact that God cannot do what is contradictory is no limit on his power; the God of traditional theism, if he exists, would still be all-powerful, even though he would be unable to do what is logically impossible.

The second proposition is 'God is all-good'; and that, as normally understood, means 'perfectly morally good'. This entails that God will always fulfil his moral obligations; for example, if he has made a promise, he will keep it; he will not cause another being to suffer except perhaps for some good purpose, and so on. And among the obligations of a perfectly good being are surely obligations to prevent and not to permit especially horrendous suffering in the world, although the extent of such obligations, and whether there are exceptions to them, are matters on which Sterba and Swinburne disagree and which will be discussed in this book. But there is more to perfect moral goodness than merely fulfilling one's obligations. Someone who throws themselves on top of a small child in order to save the child from being killed by an oncoming shell does far more than she is obliged to do, and is for that reason nearer to being a more perfect being than one who merely fulfils her obligations. A perfectly morally good being would surely always do a morally good action (even if that being does not have an obligation to do it), and where there is a best possible action which that being is able to do, always do that best possible action. Or, if there are several different actions of which a morally perfect being can do only one, as good as each other but better than any other possible action, that being would do one of those actions.

The third proposition which Mackie considered was 'there is evil', which includes both moral evils and natural evils. Moral evils are here taken to be bad states of affairs that result from or are constituted by humans intentionally causing them or through negligence allowing them to occur, that it would be prima facie wrong not to prevent. Natural evils are taken to be bad states of affairs that do not result from intentional or negligent human wrongdoing that it would also be prima facie wrong not to prevent. From which it follows that morally evil actions are actions that cause or permit the occurrence of either prima facie morally evil states of affairs or naturally evil states of affairs, and so such actions can be either merely prima facie morally evil or conclusively morally evil.

In response to Mackie's challenge, Alvin Plantinga argued[4] that it might not be feasible for God to create a world containing moral good without it also containing moral evil, given the actual free choices which humans will make. This is because moral good involves rational beings freely choosing to do good rather than evil, and moral evil involves them freely choosing to do evil rather than good; and God could not create beings who had such free choices and at the same time cause them always to make the good choice, rather than the evil choice. It has been widely held by theists and atheists alike that Plantinga essentially solved the problem of evil as Mackie had formulated it. What Plantinga seemed to have shown is that it is not within the power of the God of traditional theism to bring about a world containing moral good but no moral evil, and so the existence of at least some evil in the world raises no problem at all for the existence of that God.

While Mackie's exchange with Alvin Plantinga focused on whether God is compatible with some moral evil, James Sterba in his contribution to this book seeks to show that the degree and amount of moral evil that actually exists in our world is logically incompatible with the existence of the all-good, all-powerful God of traditional theism. In contrast, Richard Swinburne in his contribution to the book seeks to show that that degree and amount of moral evil is logically compatible with (and does not constitute powerful evidence against) the existence of the all-good, all-powerful God of traditional theism.

Clearly, humans (and the higher animals) have suffered enormously in the course of human history and continue to suffer. We are all familiar, either in our own experience or through reading newspapers or watching television, with the overwhelming evidence that vast numbers of people suffer much from physical and mental cruelty at the hands of others; and that there have been large-scale cruel persecutions of whole populations by their rulers or conquerors. The last four centuries have witnessed the slave trade, the Holocaust, and the Soviet Gulag, as well as the horrors of two world wars and innumerable small wars. All this has been in addition to the suffering caused by natural causes such as disease, starvation, and accidents.

This rightly leads any morally sensitive person to question whether the universe has been created and sustained by a perfectly good and omnipotent God. For surely, we suppose, a perfectly good God would seek to eliminate such suffering, and an omnipotent God could easily have done so. Hence, understandably, many have concluded that there is no God of that kind. This book then is a dialogue between two philosophers, one of whom (James Sterba) believes that this conclusion is correct, and the other of whom (Richard Swinburne) believes that the conclusion is not correct. Swinburne holds that despite the initial plausibility of such a conclusion, it is not logically possible for a God to remove all the world's suffering without at the same time making human and animal life far less worth living in crucial respects; and so a perfectly good and omnipotent God might well permit that suffering. In contrast, Sterba holds that that God, if he exists, would be engaging in preventing especially horrendous consequences of immoral actions in our world when no one else either would or could prevent those consequences.

However, both of us (Sterba and Swinburne) hold that there are objective moral truths discoverable by rational reflection, and thus we reject the opposing views of moral non-cognitivism and moral anti-realism. (Moral non-cognitivism holds that moral 'propositions' merely express attitudes towards states of affairs: moral anti-realism holds that, although moral propositions purport to be true, in fact, no proposition claiming that something is morally good or obligatory is true because there is no such property as moral goodness or obligatoriness.) Most importantly, the problem of evil cannot even arise without assuming an objective morality applicable to both God and ourselves.[5] Both of us also believe that the fundamental moral truths are not made true simply by God willing them to be true; and so we both reject a more radical 'divine command' theory which claims that all the fundamental moral truths are made true by the free choice of God.

Arguments between theists and atheists usually begin with the assumption that the all-good, all-powerful God of traditional theism exists. Atheists grant this assumption for the sake of argument, and then go on to claim that it is inconsistent with the existence of evil. Theists usually think they have some independent argument for the existence of that God. Both theists and atheists believe that evil exists, where evil is understood to be either moral evil or natural evil.

Beyond the assumption that the all-good, all-powerful God of traditional theism exists and that evil exists without which there would be no problem of evil, the crucial question is what additional premises are to be added to complete the argument. Either there are additional premises about what is morally required or permitted that can be added to these two assumptions that show the *compatibility* of the God of traditional theism and all the evil in the world, or there are additional premises about what is morally required or permitted that can be added to these two assumptions that show the *incompatibility* of the God of traditional theism and all the evil in the world. Which is it? That is what this debate between the two of us (Sterba and Swinburne) is all about.

Sterba's first essay was the first to be written, and Swinburne's first essay, while setting out his own view, responds to Sterba. Sterba's second essay then responds to Swinburne, while also restating Sterba's own view. Swinburne's second essay again responds to Sterba while also restating Swinburne's own view. After that, Sterba changed his second essay in the light of Swinburne's second, and this process continued until both of us were satisfied that we had done the best we could to meet the objections of the other. The reader must now judge between us.

2
The World's Evils Are Logically Incompatible with God's Existence

James Sterba

While I will be defending atheism in this debate, I have not always been an atheist. In fact, I was in a religious order for twelve years, leaving only just before I would have had to have taken final vows at age 26. And I only became an atheist recently after accepting a John Templeton grant to apply the yet untapped resources of ethics and political philosophy to the problem of evil. Work on this Templeton grant ultimately resulted in my developing the argument I will try to summarize here which is set out in more detail in my book.[1] Moreover, if anyone is successful in poking a hole in my argument, I am happy to give up being an atheist. My commitment to atheism is only as strong as the soundness and validity of my argument. Undercut my argument and poof, at least in my case, no more atheist. So, what is my argument?

I. The Argument from Moral Evil

My argument begins by considering whether there would be a justification for God's not preventing, hence permitting, the final stage of especially horrendous evil actions of wrongdoers, the stage where the wrongdoers would be imposing their evil consequences on their victims.[2] Let's assume that there would be a justification, at least in terms of freedom of the agent, for God's not interfering with the imaginings, intending, and even the taking of initial steps by wrongdoers toward bringing about especially horrendous evil consequences on their would-be victims. Let's also assume that there would be a justification, at least in terms of freedom of the agent, for God's not interfering when the consequences of immoral actions are not horrendously evil. So, the question is: Could there be a 'greater good' justification for God's permitting especially horrendous evil consequences of immoral actions?

Here it is important to see that goods that could be provided to us are of just two types. Either they are goods to which we have a right, or they are goods to which we do not have a right. That captures all the goods that could be provided to us.

Goods to Which We Have a Right

Providing us with goods to which we have a right is also a way of preventing evil. More precisely, the provision of such goods by those who could easily do so without violating anyone's rights is a way of preventing the evil of the violation of the people's rights. Thus, if I provide someone with food and lodging to which that person has a right when I alone, other than God, can easily do so without violating anyone's rights, I prevent that person from suffering an evil. Correspondingly, the non-provision of goods to which we have a right is also a way of doing evil; more precisely, the non-provision of such goods by those who could easily do so without violating anyone's rights would itself be morally evil. Thus, if I do not provide someone with the food and lodging to which that person has a right when I alone, other than God, can easily do so, without violating anyone's rights, my omission which is morally equivalent to a doing here, is also morally evil.

In addition, goods to which we are entitled and goods to which we are not entitled are either first-order goods, like the freedom not to be brutally assaulted, that do not logically presuppose that any serious wrongdoing has occurred or second-order goods, like receiving needed medical aid after having been brutally assaulted, that do logically presuppose that some serious wrongdoing has occurred.[3] Now for all first-order goods to which we have a right, the basic moral requirement that governs their provision is:

Moral Evil Prevention Requirement I
Prevent rather than permit especially horrendous evil consequences of immoral actions (a good to which we have a right) when, without violating anyone's rights, that can easily be done.

For example, if you can easily prevent a small child from starving to death or prevent your partner from being viciously assaulted without violating anyone's rights then you should do so. This requirement is an exceptionless minimal component of the Pauline Principle never to do evil that good may come of it which would be acceptable to consequentialists and non-consequentialists, as well as to theists and atheists alike.[4] This requirement would be acceptable to consequentialists and non-consequentialists because as this minimal component of the Pauline Principle has been formulated there are no good consequentialist or non-consequentialist reasons for violating it.[5] Theists and atheists also accept this requirement for the same reasons that consequentialists and non-consequentialists accept it. However, theists also believe that God, without violating this requirement, can be morally justified in permitting especially horrendous evil consequences of immoral action because they believe that that may be the only logically possible way of preventing greater evil consequences. Atheists would just love to be able to demonstrate that theists are mistaken about this.

First-Order Goods to Which We Have a Right

With respect to first-order goods to which we have a right, we are sometimes stuck in a situation where we can only provide some people with such a good and hence prevent a corresponding evil from being inflicted on them by not providing other people with another good whose non-provision inflicts a lesser evil on them. For example, we may only be able to save five people from being robbed and viciously assaulted who are close by if we don't try to also save two other people from being robbed and viciously assaulted who are farther away. God, however, would never find himself causally stuck in such situations. God would always have the causal power to prevent both evils.

Accordingly, God would have to prevent both evil consequences in all such cases unless there is a good that either does or does not logically presuppose that any serious wrongdoing has occurred that would justify God in permitting the lesser evil in such cases.[6]

Second-Order Goods to Which We Have a Right

Now with respect to second-order goods to which we have a right, like the good of life-saving medical aid after one has been brutally assaulted, it would be wrong not to provide such goods when one can easily do so without violating anyone's rights. However, given that the need we have for such goods depends on the occurrence of serious moral wrongdoing, it would be morally required for anyone who could easily do so without violating anyone's rights to prevent the consequences of that wrongdoing on which the second-order good depends. Hence, the victims of horrendous moral wrongdoing who would have a second-order right to such goods would have morally preferred that anyone who could easily have done so without violating anyone's rights would have kept them from suffering the consequences of the wrongdoing that would ground their right to any second-order goods of rectification and compensation. For example, a victim of a vicious assault would have morally preferred that anyone who could easily have done so without violating anyone's rights would have prevented the consequences of his assault to his now having the right to second-order goods resulting from that assault. So we have:

Moral Evil Prevention Requirement II
Do not permit rather than prevent the infliction of especially horrendous evil consequences of immoral actions on their would-be victims in order to provide would-be beneficiaries with goods they would morally prefer not to have.[7]

This requirement too is an exceptionless minimal component of the Pauline Principle which would be acceptable to consequentialists and non-consequentialists and it should be acceptable to theists and atheists as well. Again, this requirement would be acceptable to consequentialists and non-consequentialists because as this minimal component of the Pauline Principle has been formulated there are no good consequentialist or non-consequentialist reasons for violating it. Theists and atheists should also accept this requirement for the same reasons that consequentialists and non-consequentialists accept it. In virtue of this moral requirement, God should have acted so as to respect the moral preferences of those who would now have rights to such second-order goods, and that would have eliminated the need for those goods. But clearly this has not been done.

Now it is often thought that the greatest good that God could provide us with is friendship with himself. It is also understood that God could not just make us his friends. Thus, if God were to offer us friendship with himself, the highest sort of friendship, we must be free to accept or reject that friendship. Likewise, God must be free to offer or not offer his friendship to us. This means that God's provision of the opportunity to be friends with himself cannot be logically conditional on his permission of especially horrendous evil consequences of immoral actions. The God of traditional theism cannot be constrained in this way with respect to his offer of friendship, otherwise he would not be all-powerful and so not the God of traditional theism. Likewise, a right to a decent life, which is a first-order right, cannot be logically conditional on God's permission of especially horrendous evil consequences of immoral actions. Accordingly, our fundamental rights could never be violated by God for the sake of a good to which we would otherwise not have had a right and could have easily done without while still enjoying the opportunity to be friends with God as well as a decent life. Hence, the would-be beneficiaries would morally prefer not to be implicated in the violation of people's fundamental rights that would obtain if they were to accept such goods given that they can easily do without them while still enjoying the opportunity to be friends with God as well as to have a decent life. This then is the kind of moral preference that would-be beneficiaries would be expressing in MEPR II. It is a moral preference that it would be morally wrong for them not to have. Thus, the all-good, all-powerful God of traditional theism would have to respect those preferences and prevented rather than permitted the horrendous evil consequences of immoral action on which the provision of such goods depend. But clearly this has not been done.

Goods to Which We Do Not Have a Right

With respect to goods to which we do not have a right, not providing such goods to others, even when we could easily do so, is not morally evil. Not providing such goods to would-be beneficiaries would not be a way of wronging them. In any case, such goods are also either first-order goods that do not logically depend on serious wrongdoing, like many of the friendships we have, or second-order goods that do logically depend on the occurrence of any serious wrongdoing, like the opportunity to provide medical care to someone who has been brutally assaulted. Now for all such first-order goods to which we do not have a right, the basic moral requirement that governs the provision of them is:

Moral Evil Prevention Requirement III
Do not permit rather than prevent especially horrendous evil consequences of immoral actions (which would violate someone's rights) in order to provide would-be recipients with goods to which they do not have a right that are not logically dependent on God's permission of those consequences, when there are countless morally unobjectionable ways of providing those goods.

This requirement too is an exceptionless minimal component of the Pauline Principle which would be acceptable to consequentialists and non-consequentialists as well as to theists and atheists alike. Again, this requirement would be acceptable to consequentialists and non-consequentialists because as this minimal component of the Pauline Principle has been formulated there are no good consequentialist or non-consequentialist reasons for violating it. However, theists also believe that God, without violating this requirement, can be justified in permitting especially horrendous evil consequences of immoral action in order to provide goods to which we do not have a right because they believe that there may be no alternative way of providing these goods that is logically possible. Atheists would just love to be able to demonstrate that theists are mistaken about this.

First-Order Goods to Which We Do Not Have a Right

Now with respect to first-order goods to which we do not have a right, both God and ourselves would have numerous ways of providing people with such goods without violating anyone's rights by permitting rather than preventing especially horrendous evil consequences of immoral actions to be inflicted on them. In cases where we humans are causally constrained by lack of resources and are thus unable to provide someone with such a good without permitting the violation of the person's rights, God would never be subject to such causal constraints.

Of course, it might be objected here that, for all we know, it could just be logically impossible for God to both provide us with first-order goods to which we do not have a right and to prevent horrendous evil consequences of immoral actions from being inflicted on us, something to which we do have a right. Again, this seems to be something that sceptical theists might want to say. But as these goods have been specified, they are first-order goods to which we do not have a right. Being such first-order goods their provision does not logically depend on occurrence of any previous wrongdoing that God would have to have permitted. Hence, it would be logically possible for God to both provide us with such first-order goods to which we do not have a right while preventing horrendous evil consequences of immoral actions from being inflicted on us, something to which we do have a right. And this undercuts the objection.

Therefore, it must be the case that God can both provide us with first-order goods to which we do not have a right and prevent especially horrendous evil consequences of immoral actions from being inflicted on us, something to which we do have a right.[8] That being the case, there are no grounds at all for making the provision of first-order goods to which we do not have a right, conditional upon God's not preventing especially horrendous evil consequences of immoral actions from being inflicted on us, given that we have a right to that prevention by whomever is in a position to do so without violating anyone's rights. Thus, suppose God were to permit the horrendous consequences of a vicious assault to be inflicted on two victims to provide them with the opportunity to be good friends with each other. That opportunity to be good friends with each other is a good that is not logically dependent on God's permission of the assault (God could have provided them with the opportunity to be good friends without permitting them to be assaulted) and so that good belongs to the domain of MEPR III.

Second-Order Goods to Which We Do Not Have a Right

The very possibility of second-order goods to which we do not have a right is conditional on the occurrence of a moral wrongdoing. For example, consider the opportunity to console a rape victim. No one is entitled to be provided with such a good, and its very existence depends upon God's permission of a rape. Hence, it would be morally required for anyone who could do so without violating anyone's rights to prevent the consequences of the rape on which the second-order good of the opportunity to console the rape victim depends. Thus, the would-be beneficiaries would morally prefer not to be implicated in the violation of people's fundamental rights which would obtain if they accepted such goods, given that they can easily do without them while still enjoying the opportunity to be friends with God as well as to have a decent life. Thus, God should have acted to respect their moral preferences not to receive such goods. Even the perpetrators of such wrongful deeds, who later have the opportunity to repent and seek forgiveness would always morally prefer that God had prevented the external consequences of their immoral deeds. So, in virtue of Moral Evil Prevention Requirement II, God should have acted to respect the moral preferences of all the would-be beneficiaries of goods that are logically dependent on God's permission of especially the horrendous evil consequences of immoral actions.

In sum, all goods that could be provided to us are either goods to which we have a right or goods to which we do not have a right. Each of these types further divides into first-order goods that do not logically depend on moral wrongdoing and second-order goods that do logically depend on moral wrongdoing. With respect then to first-order goods to which we have a right and first-order goods to which we do not have a right, Moral Evil Prevention Requirement I and Moral Evil Prevention Requirement III respectively morally constrain the pursuit of greater good justifications for both God and ourselves. And with respect to second-order goods to which we have a right and second-order goods to which we do not have a right, according to Moral Evil Prevention Requirement II, the preferences of the would-be beneficiaries of such goods morally require that God prevent the first-order evil consequences on which the very existence of those second-order goods depend.

Here it might be objected that while it may seem appropriate, even required, for God not to permit rather than prevent especially horrendous evil consequences of immoral actions in any particular case, once we generalize that behaviour for all such cases, morally objectionable consequences result. Let us consider whether this is the case first with respect to first-order goods to which we have a right and then with respect to first-order goods to which we do not have a right.

The General Provision of First-Order Goods to Which We Have a Right

Thus, suppose that you had done all that you could to prevent the consequences of some horrendously evil action and you could see that you were not going to be completely successful. Suppose that at that moment God were to intervene and provide what is additionally needed to completely prevent all the evil consequences of that action. Presumably, you would be pleased that God had so intervened. Now imagine you are again considering whether to intervene to prevent the consequences of another horrendously evil action. You might reason that if you did intervene you might well be successful this time. Yet upon further reflection you might decide that there is really no need for you to intervene at all because if you do nothing, you could now assume that God would intervene as he had done before, and this time completely prevent the evil consequences from happening. So you do nothing.

Here, I claim, God would be morally required to intervene to prevent the evil consequences of that action, but in this instance, God's prevention should only be partially successful. Here is why. Originally, let's say, you were in a position to prevent the abduction of a small boy into a car. Now that you have chosen to do nothing, you witness the abductors successfully driving off with the boy. Only later do you learn that the car was subsequently stopped many miles away by a passing patrol car because it had a busted tail-light, and the small boy, whom the kidnappers had terrorized and were planned to kill was then discovered in the car and freed by the police. So, you assume, not unreasonably, that God was involved in this prevention as well as in the earlier one. Nevertheless, you cannot help but note that the intervention was not as successful as it presumably would have been if you had chosen to intervene yourself. After all, imagine that you were standing close to the boy. You could have just screamed to alert others and/or pulled the boy away and completed foiled the abductors. As a result, the boy would not have been terrorized as he was during the time he was in the hands of his abductors before the police were able to rescue him.

So, in this hypothetical world, you begin to detect a pattern in God's interventions. When you choose to intervene to prevent especially horrendously evil consequences, either you will be completely successful in preventing those consequences or your intervention will fall short. When the latter is going to happen, God does something to make the prevention completely successful. Likewise, when you choose not to intervene to prevent such consequences, God again intervenes but not in a way that is fully successful. Here there is a residue of evil consequences that the victim still does suffer. This residue is not a horrendous evil, but it is a significant one, and it is something for which you are primarily responsible. You could have prevented those consequences, but you chose not to do so and that makes you responsible for them. Of course, God too could prevent those harmful consequences from happening even if you don't. It is just that in such cases God chooses not to intervene so as to completely prevent both the significant as well as the horrendous evil consequences of wrongful actions in order to leave you with an ample opportunity for soul-making.⁹ One might think, as I would, that the God of traditional theism should prevent both the significant and the horrendous consequences of immoral actions and there would still be ample opportunity for soul-making. It is just that if God were only to prevent the horrendous evil consequences of such actions, as is all that my argument, using MEPR I–III, maintains should be done, that would clearly make the world much, much better than the world we currently inhabit, and it definitely would not turn the world into a moral kindergarten since we would be able to prevent both the significant and the horrendous consequences of immoral actions, sometimes with God's help when we chose to do so, and when we chose not to do so, we would be responsible for the significant evil consequences of those actions which we are imagining God chooses not to prevent in this case to give us more than an ample opportunity for soul-making.¹⁰ Instead of being a moral kindergarten, it would be a world that morally good people would prefer to inhabit. It is just that this would not be our world because in our world the horrendous evil consequences of immoral actions clearly abound, consequences that an all-good, all-powerful God of traditional theism, if he existed, would not have permitted.

The General Provision of First-Order Goods to Which We Have No Right

With respect to goods to which we have a right, other people generally are in a position to provide them to us. However, for first-order goods to which we do not have a right, only some people will generally be in a position to provide to them to us, and for some such goods only God would be in a position to provide them to us.

Call the first sort of goods, human-and-divine option goods and the second sort, divine-only option goods. Thus, only with respect to human-and-divine option goods could God and ourselves possibly be competing to provide them. Here God should follow a limited interventionist policy analogous to the one that I have argued that he should be following with respect to goods to which we do have a right, which fittingly are also human-and-divine option goods. By contrast, with respect to divine-only option goods, the only morally important requirement that should govern God's provision of such goods is the exceptionless minimal component of the Pauline Principle captured by Moral Evil Prevention Requirement III: Do not permit rather than prevent especially horrendous evil consequences of immoral actions (which would violate someone's rights) in order to provide would-be recipients with goods to which they do not have a right when there are countless morally unobjectionable ways of providing those goods.

Still, it might be objected that if God did intervene to the degree to which I am claiming he would have to be intervening, we would no longer be living in a world governed by natural laws, and so no longer be able to discover such laws and put that knowledge to work in our lives.[11]

Clearly, there is no denying that a world where God intervened, as needed, to prevent especially horrendous evil consequences of immoral actions would a different world from the one we currently inhabit.[12] But such a world would still have regularities. They would just be somewhat different from the regularities that hold in our world. Think of the fictional city of Metropolis in which Superman/Clark Kent was imagined to live. Surely regularities did hold in that imaginary city. They were just different from the regularities that hold in our world because of the 'to be expected' interventions of Superman that occurred in Metropolis. So, if all the world were like Metropolis, we would still discover natural laws. We would just learn that the operation of those laws was subject to moral constraints because of the additional regular interventions of God. The same would be true in an ideally just and powerful political state, where all murders, serious assaults, etc. would be prevented. There too natural law regularities would be constrained, so to speak, by the to-be-expected regular moral interventions of such a state.[13] Of course, soul-making would still exist in Metropolis or in an ideally just and powerful state, as it does in our world. It is just that the opportunities for soul-making that would exist there would be limited to just those opportunities that morally good people would prefer to have. But clearly no one should be objecting to living under those regularities.

Conclusion

This concludes our search for whether there is some greater moral good that would suffice to justify what would have to be God's widespread permission of especially horrendous consequences of immoral actions. I have argued that there is no such greater good because when that good is understood to be the prevention of a greater evil from which we have a first-order right to be protected, God could always prevent all such evils (as needed), and when the greater good is understood to be a good to which we do not have a right, God would have countless ways of providing us with such a good without violating our first-order rights. I have also argued that both kinds of second-order goods would not exist if God respected, as he should, the moral preferences of the would-be beneficiaries of those goods. In short, given our morality, primarily the Moral Evil Prevention Requirements I through III, which are morally exceptionless minimal components of the Pauline Principle, no all-good, all-powerful God is logically possible.

We can also restate my argument to approximate the form that John Mackie should have used to succeed in his famous exchange with Alvin Plantinga as follows:

(1) There is an all-good, all-powerful God. (This is assumed for the sake of argument by both Mackie and Plantinga.)
(2) If there is an all-good, all-powerful God then necessarily he would be adhering to Moral Evil Prevention Requirements I–III.
(3) If God were adhering to Moral Evil Prevention Requirements I–III, then necessarily especially horrendous evil consequences of immoral actions would not be obtaining through what would have to be his permission.
(4) Horrendous evil consequences of immoral actions do obtain all around us, which, if God exists, would have to be through his permission. (This is assumed by both Mackie and Plantinga.)
(5) Therefore, it is not the case that there is an all-good, all-powerful God, which contradicts (1).

II. The Argument from Natural Evil

Turning to the problem of natural evil, it is important to see that the problem of natural evil and the problem of moral evil are distinct problems and the solution to each of them is importantly different. Thus, with respect to natural evil in our world, it is not possible to avoid all significant natural evil. When a serious flood occurs the would-be victims of the flood and the scavengers who would survive by feeding on their dead bodies are in conflict in our world. One or the other will suffer death. However, with respect to moral evil of the significant and especially horrendous sort, the situation is different. Except for lifeboat cases, individual human beings are not in unavoidable life-and-death conflict with each other. With respect to most of the conflicts we have, morality imposes its demands on each of us such that it is possible for us all to live decent lives together, without anyone doing anything that is especially horrendously morally evil, thereby imposing significant or horrendous evil consequences on others. This is why it would be possible and morally required of God to prevent especially horrendous evil consequences of our immoral actions, as needed, at the same time that it would not be possible, and so not morally required of God, to prevent all the significant or even horrendous evil consequences of natural evil in our world. Nevertheless, with respect to natural evil, God would be under a further obligation to prevent especially horrendous consequences of natural evil, as needed, to limit serious harm in the world. Moreover, because meeting the basic needs of human beings over those of other species who do not suffer as intensely as we do is the best way to limit serious suffering in our world, there is a moral rationale for favouring the basic needs of human beings over those of non-human sentient and non-sentient living beings. Likewise, a similar moral rationale supports favouring the basic needs of non-human sentient beings over those of non-sentient living beings, and a similar moral rationale favours limiting harm to non-sentient living beings when their interests do not conflict with those of any other living beings. Hence, this hierarchy of moral rationales is incorporated into the following Natural Evil Prevention Requirements.

Natural Evil Prevention Requirements

(I) Prevent, rather than permit, especially horrendous evil consequences of natural evil from being inflicted on rational beings (a good to which they have a right), as needed, when one can easily do so without causing greater or comparable harm to other rational beings.

(II) Do not permit, rather than prevent, especially horrendous evil consequences of natural evil to be inflicted on rational beings (which would violate their rights) simply to provide them with goods they would morally prefer not to have.

(III) Do not permit, rather than prevent, especially horrendous evil consequences of natural evils from being inflicted on rational beings (which would violate their rights) in order to provide them with goods to which they do not have a right, when there are countless morally unobjectionable ways of providing those goods to rational beings.

(IV) Prevent, rather than permit, especially horrendous evil consequences of natural evil from being inflicted on non-rational sentient beings, as needed, whenever the welfare of rational beings is not at stake and one can easily do so without causing greater or comparable harm to other non-rational sentient life.

(V) Do not permit, rather than prevent, especially horrendous evil consequences of natural evil to be inflicted on non-rational sentient beings simply to provide rational beings with goods they would morally prefer not to have.

(VI) Do not permit, rather than prevent, especially horrendous evil consequences of natural evils from being inflicted on non-rational sentient beings whenever the welfare of rational beings is not at stake in order to provide non-rational sentient beings with goods not required for their basic welfare, when there are countless morally unobjectionable ways of providing those goods to non-rational sentient beings.

(VII) Prevent, rather than permit, especially horrendous evil consequences of natural evil from being inflicted on non-sentient living beings, as needed, whenever the welfare of rational and non-rational sentient beings is not at stake, and one can easily do so without causing greater or comparable harm to other non-sentient life.[14]

(VIII) Do not permit, rather than prevent, especially horrendous evil consequences of natural evil to be inflicted on non-sentient living beings simply to provide rational beings with goods they would morally prefer not to have.

(IX) Do not permit, rather than prevent, especially horrendous evil consequences of natural evils from being inflicted on non-sentient living beings whenever the welfare of rational and non-rational sentient beings is not at stake in order to provide non-sentient living beings with goods not required for their basic welfare, when there are countless morally unobjectionable ways of providing those goods to non-sentient living beings.

Now at least for horrendous consequences of natural evil, NEPR I–IX apply first to political states, and only when those states either cannot, or wrongfully do not, meet them, do they apply to the individuals, particularly but not exclusively, to the individuals who are responsible for the actions of those states, and only when such individuals either cannot, or wrongfully do not, meet the requirements, do they then apply to God. What this order of application ensures is that as much soul-making obtains as possible consistent with meeting these exceptionless minimal natural evil requirements.

It also should be pointed out here that God's interventions to prevent the consequences of especially horrendous natural evil would have a law-like regularity to them. This means that God's intervention to prevent evil consequences in any one case would demand his intervention in all other similar cases. Moreover, the same holds true for political states and their members. Their obligation to prevent evil consequences (including both natural and moral) also has a law-like regularity, such that an obligation in one case implies an obligation in other similar cases. Of course, in the case of God, it is the absence of any law-like prevention of especially horrendous consequences of natural evil in our world, as needed, that is logically incompatible with God's existence.

III. Restrictions on Wrongdoing

I have argued that the God of traditional theism, if he exists, should be engaged in a wide-ranging policy of preventing rather than permitting especially horrendous consequences of wrongdoing that are inflicted on ourselves and other living beings which is clearly not occurring. But what about wrongdoing directed at God himself? Shouldn't I be maintaining that God, if he exists, should be preventing the consequences of wrongdoing that are directed at God himself? Actually, my view here is just the opposite. The God of traditional theism, if he exists, should not prevent the consequences of wrongful acts that are directed simply at himself. This is because if the all-powerful God of traditional theism exists, he would be invulnerable to serious harm from our wrongful acts directed at himself. Given then that God himself could not be so harmed by our wrongful acts, God would have good reason to fully respect our freedom in this regard by not preventing the consequences of these actions that are directed simply at himself, while still maintaining that such wrongdoing requires rectification.

Of course, it could be argued that when we harm the creatures that God is assumed to have brought into the world, we would be harming God as well in just the way that we would normally harm the parents of a child by harming the child. Yet, if God is truly all-powerful then he cannot by creating be made vulnerable in the way that we can be made vulnerable by procreating. So, God, if he is truly the all-powerful God of traditional theism, cannot be harmed in this way, although we can.

Now St Anselm once argued that since God is an infinite being, all of our wrongdoing against God has infinite disvalue creating a debt that requires something of comparable positive value if it is to be repaid.[15] But if our wrongdoing against God actually causes no serious harm to God at all, then such acts could not be the source of infinite disvalue to God.

Thus, it is when our wrongdoing is directed at human and non-human living creatures that MEPR I–III and NEPR I–IX apply requiring God to restrict our horrendous evil consequences. However, when our wrongdoing is directed at God himself because he cannot be seriously harmed at all by our actions, the God of traditional theism should not be restricting our freedom at all with respect those actions. Rather, our freedom to engage in wrongdoing directed simply at God should be completely unrestricted which is still compatible with maintaining that such wrongdoing requires rectification.

IV. Ethics after Creation

It is important to realize that my case against God with respect to moral and natural evil has nothing to do with speculation as to whether God could have created a different world with different beings in it that suffer less than us or are happier than us or any such comparison. Before God creates, he is not under any obligation to anyone. Nor would it benefit anyone, not even himself, to create, or not to create one particular world rather than any other. Moreover, provided that the creatures in the world that God creates are better off existing than not existing given their natural capacities, no one would be harmed by God's creating that particular world rather than any other. After creation, however, God would have an obligation to benefit and protect those he did create, but that obligation is grounded in the needs of the creatures he actually brought into existence. So, it is only after creation that God's options become constrained by what is for the good of the beings he created. Hence, given that creatures that exist in this world are almost all, as far as we can tell, better off existing than not existing, there is no argument against the existence of God that can be based on creation. That is why my argument is based on what God would have to be doing after creation because only then would God through his actions be benefiting or harming the creatures he presumptively has made. Notice that something like this obtains for ourselves with respect to the procreation of our own children.

V. Not a Moral Agent

In the introduction to this book, Richard Swinburne and I agreed that in calling the God of traditional theism all-good we understand his goodness to include moral goodness. While this is the view held by the greater majority of theologians and philosophers working on the problem of evil today, there are some theologians and philosophers who maintain that the God of traditional theism is all-good but not morally good because they deny that God is a moral agent. Brian Davies is best known for his defence of this view, and in my book on the problem of evil, I devote a chapter to Davies's view. More recently, however, another Brian, Brian Huffling, has restated and added new support for Davies's view.[16] So here I want to show why even when supported with Huffling's new work, Davies's view still leads to a God who is not logically possible.

Now Huffling claims that the view he shares with Davies can be supported by the following argument.

> First premise: If God is the creator of the universe, then he does not have the property of creation.
> Second premise: Morality is a property of creation.
> Conclusion: Therefore, God does not have moral properties—he is not a moral being.

To evaluate Huffling's argument, let's keep the first premise and substitute for the second—Intelligence is a property of creation. Now Huffling does not want to draw the conclusion that God does not have the property of intelligence—that he is not an intelligent being. In fact, elsewhere Huffling affirms that intelligence is an analogical property possessed by both God and ourselves.[17] In addition, he affirms that God is rich in mercy toward us, that he loves us, and that he is virtuous, all of which are to be understood to be analogical properties possessed by both God and ourselves. But why then cannot being morally good also be understood to be an analogical property that is possessed by God and ourselves? Huffling provides no reason to distinguish this property from the other properties that he thinks are analogical properties possessed by both God and ourselves.

Huffling wants to hold that God is good in virtue of what he is but not in virtue of he does. Given that being morally good is thought to have implications for what one does, this may explain why Huffling holds that the property of being morally good is not possessed by God. The problem with Huffling's view here is that elsewhere he claims that other properties that hold analogically of God such as being rich in mercy, loving, and virtuous are also properties that have implications for what one does. So Huffling is left with no consistent way of distinguishing the property of being morally good from other properties that he thinks are analogically possessed by God.

Now the one property that Huffling is most concerned to deny that it is possessed by God is that of having obligations. Here no doubt some clarification is required. When we say that we ourselves have obligations or are under moral obligations, we usually understand ourselves to be pulled to act in the way that our obligations prescribe at the same time that we find ourselves to some degree being pulled to act in opposing ways as well with the result that we sometimes end up doing what we clearly know to be morally wrong.

Nevertheless, obligations are usually understood to work differently for God. God, it is thought, can fulfil his moral obligations to us without any of the struggle we experience. In God's case, what God ought to do and what is in his interest to do are always the same because God's interests never pull against what would fairly serve all relevant interests, or at least this would be so if God were an all-good, all-powerful being. But this is just the way analogies work. Not everything that is true when an analogical term is applied to one analogate is also true when the term is applied to other analogates. Thus, while it is true that for us obligations frequently pull us to act one way at the same time that we find ourselves being pulled to act in other ways, this is not the case for God.

Moreover, we can greatly simplify the use of analogy at work here by replacing talk of obligations altogether with talk of what would be good for a person, such as God, to do and bad for him not to do. We can also do the same with talk of moral goodness, replacing it with talk of what is good overall with respect to a person's actions and their effects on others. Surely these greatly simplified uses of analogy would apply to the God of traditional theism if the other uses that theists accept are thought to succeed in doing so.

When we apply predicates to God and ourselves (even the predicate of being metaphysically good), claiming our assertions are true, we have to be speaking analogically. Even metaphorical statements made about God such as the Psalmist's claim that The Lord is my rock, my fortress, and my deliverer (or statements made by scientists that the atom is like our solar system claiming that its nucleus is like the sun and its electrons are like the planets orbiting around the sun) which also purport to be true have to be conveying their truth, when they are true, through non-literal, analogical language.

Huffling also uses the following argument to support Davies's view:

> First premise: If God were morally good, he would have to be subject to moral norms.
> Second premise: God is not dependent on or subject to anything.
> Conclusion: Hence, God is not subject to moral norms.

Here we need to ask if God is not subject to moral norms what is his relationship to them? Now it might be useful to approach this question by asking what is God's relationship to other analogous norms or truths such as those found in mathematics or logic. For example, consider the law of identity in logic or the arithmetical truth that $2+2=4$. What is God's relationship to them? Wouldn't God, like ourselves, just know them to be true? Surely it doesn't make sense to ask who makes the law of identity or $2+2=4$ to be true. Similarly, in morality it doesn't seem to make sense to ask who makes the moral norm 'Don't torture infants for fun of it' true. Rather than by being caused to be true, it looks like each of these claims is properly said to be justified by appeal to the ultimate axioms or norms of the domain to which it belongs. Thus, in morality, torturing infants for the fun of it is wrong because it is a clear violation of morality's most basic norm to treat all relevant interests fairly. If any further moral justification for this claim were needed, that is it; nothing else is required. I don't think this means that we are dependent on the norms or axioms of logic, mathematics, or morality, but it does mean we are subject to them.

It is also important to point out that I have taken up this Davies/Huffling perspective here in order to show that the atheism that I defend against Swinburne cannot be costlessly avoided by simply adopting the Davies/Huffling perspective. Not surprisingly, Swinburne is doing something similar. He also is not just interested in refuting my view by showing that God is logically possible given all the evil in the world. He is also trying to show that God is more likely than not in order to refute those atheists who only endorse evidential arguments from evil against the existence of the God of traditional theism.

VI. Limited God

Yet might it not help to avoid the conclusion of my argument against the existence of an all-good, all-powerful God to hypothesize a limited god? This has been an option favoured by, among others, Alfred North Whitehead and Charles Hartshorne.[18] Unfortunately, such a god would have to be either extremely immoral or extremely weak. Such a god would either have to be extremely immoral, more immoral than all of our historical villains taken together, because he would have permitted all the horrendous evil consequences of those villains when he could easily have prevented them without permitting a greater evil or failing to provide us with some greater good. Alternatively, such a god, while morally good, would have to be extremely weak either because he is logically incapable of preventing the evil consequences that we are only causally incapable of preventing or because he is logically incapable of providing us with goods to which we are not entitled without permitting us to suffer especially horrendous evil consequences of immoral actions, something that we ourselves are only sometimes causally incapable of doing. Surely then no useful purpose would be served by hypothesizing such a limited god who would either *be so much more evil* than all our greatest villains or, while moral, would *be so much less powerful* than ourselves.

VII. Summing Up

Here are the most fundamental elements of my argument:

Most Fundamental Elements
(I) All goods that could be provided to us are either goods to which we have a right or goods to which we do not have a right.
(II) Each of these types further divides into first-order goods that do not logically depend on moral wrongdoing and second-order goods that do logically depend on moral wrongdoing.
(III) With respect to first-order goods to which we have a right and first-order goods to which we do not have a right, Moral Evil Prevention

Requirement I and Moral Evil Prevention Requirement III respectively morally constrain the pursuit of greater-good justifications for both God and ourselves.

(IV) And with respect to second-order goods to which we have a right and second-order goods to which we do not have a right, according to Moral Evil Prevention Requirement II, the preferences of the would-be beneficiaries of such goods morally require that God prevent the first-order evil consequences on which the very existence of those second-order goods depend.

(V) Morally good people would not object to God's universal imposition of Moral Evil Prevention Requirements I–III, as needed. Morally bad people would object, but no one would be morally required to take their objections into account in this regard.

(VI) Natural Evil Prevention Requirements I–IX would have to be met by God analogously to the way Moral Evil Prevention Requirements I–III have to be met.

(VII) These evil preventions have not generally occurred in our world which is logically incompatible with the existence of the all-good, all-powerful God of traditional theism.

Now the conclusion of my argument is that that the all-good, all-powerful God of traditional theism is logically incompatible with all the evil in the world. As it turns out, most atheists have not claimed to have such a strong argument for their view. Most atheists have thought that the best they could hope to show is that the God of traditional theism is unlikely, maybe very unlikely, given what we know about the world, particularly what we know about the amount of evil in it; they have not though they could establish anything more than this.

Of course, John Mackie had tried to establish something much stronger. Mackie had tried to show that the God of traditional theism was logically incompatible with the evil in the world. To do this, he had proposed what he thought were two necessary metaphysical/moral principles which when cojoined with the fact that there was evil in the world would entail the non-existence of the God of traditional theism. However, in his exchange with Alvin Plantinga, Plantinga was able to show that Mackie's metaphysical/moral principles were not the necessary principles they would have to be for his argument to work. Even before Mackie himself conceded the failure of his argument in *The Miracle of Theism* published in 1983, philosophers who wanted to defend atheism, seemingly unaware of any suitable logically necessary metaphysical or moral premises waiting in the wings that could be deployed, turned their attention to a new strategy—that of developing an explicitly evidential argument for atheism that did not utilize necessary metaphysical or moral premises. It is this approach that has generally characterized arguments for atheism that have been offered from the time that Mackie's argument failed to the present day.

As a result, it was only in 2019 with significant assistance from an earlier Templeton grant that I was able to draw on yet untapped resources from moral and political philosophy to come up with minimal, but logically necessary, moral requirements of the Pauline Principle to formulate the Mackie-style logical argument against the existence of the God of traditional theism that I have set out in this essay. Given my religious background, I wanted the strongest possible argument against the existence of the God of traditional theism before I committed myself to atheism. This meant I wanted an argument based on logically necessary requirements rather than on just probabilistic ones. The argument that I have presented in this essay is just such an argument. It is on the soundness and validity of that argument that my commitment to atheism rests.

3
The World's Evils Are Logically Compatible with God's Existence

Richard Swinburne

From as early a period of my life as I can recall, I have always believed that God exists—because of influences which I cannot recall. Then in my teenage years I became aware that many people, including myself, need reasoned arguments in order to justify this belief. And when I began to study philosophy, and in particular the philosophy of science, I came to realize that the most general features of the universe, to which the achievements of modern science direct our attention, provide strong positive evidence for the existence of a perfectly good God; and I have subsequently argued for this view in various places.[1] But the existence of much evil in the world has always provided a very important argument against the existence of such a God. So I began to reflect on what sort of humans such a God might make and in what kind of world he might put them; and I came to the conclusion that he might well make imperfect humans and put them in an imperfect world, but one in which humans could (with God's help) make themselves more perfect humans and their world a more perfect world—if they so chose; and that such a world might well contain the substantial amount of evil that occurs in our world.[2] I hope that readers will not think me callous in supposing that there could be a moral justification for a God to allow the horrible evils that occur in our world. I hope that I am not callous, and that I do care very much about the evils which so many humans endure. But James Sterba's essay seems to me to have far too limited a view of what the goodness of a human life would consist in, and of the moral right of a God who created us to make it possible for us freely to choose to have or not to have such a life on earth and after our earthly life. I shall argue that if God is to make it possible for us to have such a free choice, it is not logically possible for him to prevent the world's actual evils. I shall argue for my view on the basis of moral intuitions which many humans, religious and non-religious, share; but I shall from time to time point out that these views are consonant with some of the teaching of Jesus and its development in the teaching of the Christian church—which is not to deny that they may be consonant also with some of the teaching of some other religions.

I. The Nature and Limits of Human Moral Rights

The concept of a moral 'right', and in particular of a human moral right, is central to Sterba's argument, and so I need to devote this first section of my response to Sterba's first essay to making some important general points about the nature of moral rights. Rights include both 'privileges' to do actions, and 'claims' to be provided with benefits. That A has a privilege to *do x* means that A has no obligation not to *do x*. In that sense, I have the right to go for a walk iff I have no obligation not to go for a walk ('iff' means 'if and only if'). That A has a claim to Z means that someone else has an obligation to provide A with Z. In that sense, I have the right to be paid for my work iff someone else (my employer) has an obligation to pay me for my work. Moral rights are rights analysable in terms of moral obligations, to be distinguished from legal rights which are rights analysable in terms of obligations enforceable by the laws of a State—though these laws often make moral rights also into legal rights, by making it legally obligatory for someone to ensure the observance of those moral rights. Our concern in this book is mainly with human moral rights (but in my second essay I shall apply my arguments briefly to animal moral rights).

The Universal Declaration of Human Rights (henceforward 'UDHR') approved by the General Assembly of the United Nations in 1948 contained a long list of 'human rights'. Because it clearly considered that these were human moral rights independently of whether they subsequently became also legal rights, they provide useful examples of rights which many have considered to be moral rights. I shall illustrate some of my subsequent points by taking examples from this list and pointing out qualifications which need to be made to them before they can correctly be judged to be moral rights. I take my examples from this list, although they may not all be ones which Sterba considers to be human rights, since Sterba gives relatively few examples of what he considers to be rights and no general account of how to determine whether a purported right is a right; but it seems to me that these are the kinds of moral rights which Sterba would recognize. The most basic human moral right is surely a privilege, the right to do any action which does not hurt (= impose evil on) anyone else—in the absence of anyone else's right to curtail our exercising that right. I will call this right our fundamental right. Lists of moral rights, I suggest, list some of the actions which, they claim, do not impose evil on anyone else and have not been curtailed by anyone who has the right to curtail them; as well as claims, rights to goods which we have in virtue of others having obligations to provide them for us.

Sterba seems to acknowledge (ch. 2 note 6, 134) that some individual or group A has a moral right only if some other individual or group B has a moral obligation to allow A to do some action, or to provide some good for A. But his discussion seems to assume that if A has a moral right, and B is able easily to satisfy it, then (unless another person C does so) necessarily B has an obligation to do so. But that seems false. A may have a right to some good, and so some particular person B may have an obligation to provide it, while no one else has any obligation to provide it, even if they can do so easily, if B does not provide it. (In virtue of the general human obligation that humans should fulfil their promises) if you have promised to pay me £100, I have a right to receive £100 from you and you have an obligation to give it to me. But if you fail to do this, it may not be anyone else's obligation to give it to me or to make you give it to me. Moral rights exist only because others have obligations to satisfy them, but not every right is such that everyone who can easily do so has an obligation or even the right to satisfy it.

Most of the rights listed in UDHR are ones which, it is generally recognized (though not stated in UDHR), some authority has the right to curtail in certain circumstances. The only authorities which I shall consider are the main ones—State, parents, and God. (I shall use 'State' to denote an independent political jurisdiction; and 'state' to denote a state of affairs.) These authorities have such rights over us because they are our major benefactors and provide gifts of great importance for us, subject to some condition on how we should use these gifts. Other would-be benefactors give us gifts which we are able to accept or refuse; and if they make their gifts subject to some explicit condition, it is only if we accept the gift (and so they become our benefactors) that we have an obligation to fulfil the condition. But the State, our parents, and (if he exists) God give us gifts subject to some implicit condition on how we should use the gifts, long before we are old enough to be able to refuse them. So, if the gifts really are good gifts essential for our existence and flourishing, I suggest that our previous use of them, as well as our continuing use of them, gives us a serious obligation to fulfil the condition (if necessary, by enduring some suffering) – so long as it does not involve doing any otherwise wrong action; and gives the benefactor the right to compel us to endure the necessary suffering.

Thus a State which has provided us with security and a moderately just legal system, without which we would be unlikely to live nearly as long as we do, does so implicitly subject to the condition that we obey its laws. Thereby it curtails rights which we would otherwise have in virtue of our fundamental right to do what we choose as long as it does not harm anyone else. For example, it is generally recognized that the State has the right to imprison humans convicted of a serious offence and so to curtail the rights of certain humans to 'liberty' (a right mentioned in UDHR Article 3). It also has the right to impose taxes, and so to curtail our right to do what we choose with our own money.

Parents (who are not merely biological parents but nurturing parents) are our greatest earthly benefactors. Parents (and especially our mothers who have borne us in their womb for nine months) have been the means by which we have come into existence, and they have devoted much time and energy to helping us to live good lives by feeding us, providing for our education, and so on. All this gives our parents a substantial right to compel us (while we are still children) to use the gifts which they have had a role in providing, in particular ways which would otherwise not be obligatory, and thus to curtail rights which we would otherwise have. Among many rights listed in UDHR which, it is generally recognized, parents have the right to curtail are 'the right to freedom of movement and residence' (Article 13), and 'the right to leave any country' (Article 13). And obviously children have many detailed obligations to obey their parents in various ways, such as to attend a certain school and do domestic tasks; and so parents have the right to curtail the fundamental right of children to do what they choose as long as it does not harm anyone else.

There is also another reason why parents have the right to curtail the rights of their children. This is that the fundamental right to do any action which does not hurt (= impose evil on) anyone else, is a right which is good for someone to have only insofar as they have some understanding of what doing the action involves, and can choose freely to do it or not to do it. Clearly, in making the choice of which actions to do, children are less well-informed than their parents about the consequences of their actions, and in general less free than their parents in that they are often moved to do particular actions by emotions which they cannot control. It is good that freer and better informed parents should make the significant choices for young children who are incapable of making sufficiently informed choices for themselves. But the older the child, the freer and better informed they are, and so the fewer the choices that parents have the right to make for them. It is for a similar reason that the State has a limited right to stop adults doing serious harm to themselves or committing suicide, when they are incapable of making serious free informed choices for themselves.

If there is a God, he is the ultimate cause (at each moment) of the existence of the law-governed physical world in which we can make significant choices, and of the existence of our parents and the State, and of their having the power and some inclination to do what they do for us. While our parents have some free will in deciding whether or not to have a child, they cannot decide who the child will be—God could have brought into existence from our parents' genes a different child from the one who actually came into existence. So God is by far our greatest benefactor. Also, being omniscient, God who knows all that it is logically possible to know (that is, in my view, everything with the exception of our future free choices), will know with far greater certainty than we can the nature and consequences of our different choices. It follows that his ~~His~~ gift of life to us is subject to the implicit condition that he has the right to curtail our rights in various ways to a far greater extent than do our lesser benefactors.

So I distinguish between what I shall call 'N-rights', 'G-rights', 'S-rights', and 'P-rights'. I define a 'N-right' as one which no one, not even God, has the right to curtail; a 'G-right' as one which God has the right to curtail; a 'P-right' as one which parents have the right to curtail; and a 'S-right' as one which the State has the right to curtail. Because God is the ultimate cause (at each moment) of our other benefactors being benefactors, and knows far better than they do the consequences of human actions, I suggest that all S-rights and P-rights are also G-rights.

Further, I suggest for the same two reasons, there are many G-rights which are not P-rights, or S-rights. Just as parents or the State who give us limited gifts have limited rights to impose burdens on some children or citizens for their benefit or the benefit of other children or citizens, God gives us the whole enormous gift of life and flourishing subject to the implicit understanding that he has a much less limited right to impose burdens on some humans for their benefit or the benefit of others. He imposes physical burdens on humans by designing the natural processes which have this effect and by giving humans 'libertarian free will', in ways which I will be exploring at length . But it also follows that God's commands to humans impose moral obligations on them which they would not otherwise have.[3] According to the Gospels, Jesus on behalf of God prescribed a way of living for all humans, which went far beyond what is required by normal human obligations, for example teaching that everyone should forgive those who seek their forgiveness (Luke 17:3–4).[4]

But of course there are limits to the rights of parents and the State to impose burdens, physical or moral, on us. For example, UDHR Article 9, 'no one shall be subjected to arbitrary arrest, detention, or exile', is clearly directed against the State, and so—to my mind, correctly—claims that the right not to be so subjected is not an S-right. I suggest that, as State and parents derive their authority from their being our benefactors, one general principle governing the limits of the authority of parents and the

State is that they must remain on balance benefactors: that is, they must always provide more good for each of us than the evils they impose upon us. It is not very easy to weigh the good against the evil, but examples illustrate in a rough way the kind of considerations which are relevant. The provision of security and a reasonably just legal system is an enormous benefit, which gives the State which provides it a considerable right to impose significant taxes, more than are needed for that provision, but only a certain amount more. If the State imposed very heavy taxes, most of which were spent on providing palaces and a luxurious lifestyle for its officials, it would cease to be on balance a benefactor. So too if it failed to provide adequate security, or if the legal system which it supports was totally corrupt. In these cases it would cease to be on balance a benefactor, and so its citizens would cease to have a moral obligation to obey its laws. And parents who provide little food and shelter and no love do not have much, if any, right to impose burdens on their children.

The general point which I am making is that there is no fixed timeless list of human rights. Which rights humans have depends, as well as on the obligations of others to provide some benefit for them, on the extent to which their fundamental right has been curtailed by parents or the State (within the limits of their moral right to do this), and so above all on whether or not there is a God and the extent to which he has curtailed their rights.

The rights possessed by the State or parents, in virtue of their being on balance benefactors does not require them to be benefactors for each period of the beneficiary's life, but on balance over the whole of the beneficiary's life (or, in the case of parents for the whole of the child's non-adult life). Consider parents living in a war zone where there are no anaesthetics available, with a newborn child whom they allow to have a serious painful operation, without which the child will die. Up until the end of the operation that child's life would be on balance a bad life, one such that it would have been better if the child had not lived. But, given that the parents would predictably give the child a good subsequent life, the parents would have had the right to impose on the child the suffering of the painful operation. Perhaps they would also have had the right to impose on one newborn child a painful operation to transplant a kidney from that child, to that child's twin in order to save the life of the latter—so long as subsequently they give the former child a good life.

The same principle—that a benefactor only has the right to curtail the rights of a beneficiary (including causing or allowing them to suffer), if the benefactor remains on balance a benefactor (in providing more good than evil) for the beneficiary—must apply to God. I will call this principle 'good benefactor condition I', 'GBC I'. But its consequences for God are very different from its consequences for parents or the State, in view of the difference made by God's almost total responsibility for our existence, and the extent of his ability to give us a good life after death. God being perfectly good will ensure that—insofar as the choice depends on him and not on our free choice—the life of each of us is on balance a good life. I understand by 'a good life', 'an overall good life', one in which the good exceeds the evil. And in writing 'creatures that exist in this world are almost all, as far as we can tell, better off existing than not existing' (ch2, 24), Sterba would seem to admit that—if God exists—he does ensure just that for almost all of us. My own view is that Sterba has exaggerated, and I shall rely simply on a modified claim that a large majority of humans on earth are, as far as we can tell, better off existing than not existing. But what of the small minority whose life on earth is such that it would have been better that they had not lived? It follows that God has an obligation to compensate them with a good life after death, and that in virtue of his omnipotence and perfect goodness, he will do so. While most religions, including Christianity, which affirm that there will be life after death, claim that the kind of life humans will have after death depends on the kind of person they are or the deeds they have done on earth (an issue which I shall discuss in section IV), nevertheless there is also a strain which claims that a miserable life on earth will find compensation in the afterlife. See for example Jesus's parable of Lazarus and the rich man (Luke 16: 19:4 1), where the kind of life Lazarus has after death is a compensation for his miserable life on earth, and yet there is no suggestion that Lazarus was a particularly good man. Hence unless Sterba can show that God does not provide a good life after death for these unfortunates, it follows from (my amended version of) Sterba's admission that he has not shown that in this respect God exceeds his rights as a benefactor.

But the onus is on Sterba to show that the unfortunates will not have a life after death—for this reason. If a hypothesis can be shown to explain a large majority of applicable cases, and the hypothesis also provides a good explanation of why it cannot be tested in certain cases, then it is reasonable to assume that it also applies in those cases, unless shown otherwise. Theism, the hypothesis that there is a God, can provide a good explanation for why a large majority of humans are better off existing than not existing; and it can also provide a good explanation of why it cannot be tested whether these unfortunates do have a good life after death. This latter explanation is that if God made it evident to everyone that there is life after death, the suspicion of most humans (and conviction of many humans) that there is no such life would not have the beneficial effect which it does have. This beneficial effect is that we can do acts which, we suspect, may have an ultimate significance which they would not have if we knew beyond reasonable doubt that there is life after death. Choices between killing someone or not killing someone, and between sacrificing our own life to save the lives of others or not doing so, would not be the serious choices which they are if humans knew beyond reasonable doubt that there is life after death. So if the hypothesis of theism is true and God seeks to give us choices of such deep significance, he will not make it possible for us to test (and so show conclusively) whether or not there is life after death—although evidence making probable the hypothesis of theism will make it probable that at least these particular unfortunates do have a life after death.[5] Since the hypothesis of theism can explain why the lives of the large majority of us on earth are on balance worth living, and it can explain why we cannot test directly (by looking at their after-death lives) whether that hypothesis applies to this small class of cases, it is reasonable to assume that it applies to them—unless Sterba can show otherwise. But I do not rely on Sterba's admission for my claim that the lives of a large majority of humans on earth are on balance good lives, and I shall seek to show the plausibility of this claim by pointing out the very good features of so many human lives and the good involved in almost all the evils which we suffer on earth, in section III.

There is, however, I suggest, a further condition on a benefactor's right to impose evils on another person, additional to GBC I, the condition that the benefactor must remain on balance a benefactor. This second condition is that no one has the right to cause or help to cause anyone to suffer any curtailment of their rights, and so any evil at all, unless doing so makes possible a comparable good (which they cannot cause in any other morally permissible way), either for that person or for someone else. I will call this second condition 'good benefactor condition II', 'GBC II'.

Many readers might agree that a parent or the State has a right (within limits) to cause or help to cause suffering to their children or citizens for the good of those children or citizens. But they might not initially agree with my claim that they have a right to cause or help to cause such suffering for the benefit, not of the sufferer, but of others. However, I suggest, there are plenty of examples to illustrate the point that parents or the State do have the right to impose suffering on some for the benefit of others. Parents surely do have the right to send a child to a neighbourhood school which she would not enjoy, rather than to another school which she would enjoy, simply in order to cement neighbourhood relations—within limits of course of the degree of suffering caused and the amount of time for which it lasts. The State obviously has the right to tax the rich, simply for the benefit of the poor. And the strongest example of the State's right to impose suffering on someone for the benefit of others is that, in a war against a tyrannous aggressor, the State has the right to impose conscription on young adults (who would otherwise leave the country) and send them to the front line where they are likely to suffer injury or death, solely for the benefit of the rest of the population.

My two GBC conditions are concerned only with the rights of benefactors, unlike Sterba's three MEPR conditions (only two of which I accept) which are supposedly binding on all rational beings. GBC II requires a careful definition of 'comparable good'.[6] There is often nothing wrong in someone doing an action which it is probable will produce a good state, but which is such that there is a small probability that it will produce a very evil state. For example, there is nothing wrong with a physician prescribing a drug, which provides the only possible and normally successful way of curing some serious illness, even if there is a small probability that it will kill the patient. So, I suggest, loosely, that a perfectly good agent will only do an action which makes possible the occurrence of an evil state, so long as it is probable that the resulting state will contain more good than evil, and that the agent cannot produce the good without permitting the possible occurrence of the evil. We should understand by an agent causing or helping to cause an evil which makes possible 'a comparable good', causing or helping to cause the occurrence of an evil where this condition is fulfilled. (See note 6 for a more precise formal definition of this condition.) The comparable good state may itself consist of a number of separate good states. Even if an agent is not justified in causing or helping to cause some evil which makes possible one such state, he may be justified in bringing about the evil in order to make possible all of them together.

But of course, while the physician may not be able to cure the patient without administering the drug, God could do so. The only actions which God cannot do, are those which are logically impossible (that is, ones the description of which entails a contradiction). The only plausible example of a kind of state which God would cause or help to cause without knowing for certain what the consequence would be when God causes some agent to have a free choice in the sense of a 'libertarian free choice'. An agent has a libertarian free choice iff their choice depends only on the agent at the time of choosing, despite their various desires influencing (but not causally determining) them to make one choice rather than another one. (Human desires are normally caused by events in their brains, and so less directly by their genes, their upbringing, and their environment.) So such a choice is not causally determined by God or anything else, other than the agent himself or herself. But God can know the relative strengths of those desires which influence agents and so the probabilities of the different choices, and so whether it is probable that some free choice will lead to more good than evil.

Hence, I suggest that the two conditions, both necessary for God to be a perfectly good benefactor are that he remains on balance a benefactor during the lives of those he creates (GBC I); and that he only causes or helps to cause an evil state if it is not logically possible that he can cause a comparable good state (for the sufferer or someone else) in any other morally permissible way (GBC II). I shall argue in section III that almost all the world's evils are such that causing or helping to cause them to occur, is a logically necessary condition for the occurrence of an actual comparable good for humans on earth. I shall, however, acknowledge that a very few of the world's evils are such that causing or helping to cause them may not make possible a comparable good for humans on earth. I shall then argue in section IV that God causing or helping to cause those evils is a logically necessary condition for the occurrence of a comparable good for many humans after their earthly death; and that a perfectly good God might well impose even those particular evils for the sake of the great good which they make possible. Hence I shall claim that the world's evils are not merely compatible with the existence of God, but do not make his existence significantly improbable.

First, however, I shall devote section II to applying the results of this section I about human rights, to dissecting Sterba's detailed claims in his first essay about such rights, and showing their very considerable limitations.

II. Sterba's Evil Prevention Requirements

Sterba's arguments are centred on his three 'moral evil prevention requirements', and their corresponding 'natural evil prevention requirements'. I assume that a moral 'requirement' is a moral obligation. Despite the fact that it is not contained in his statement of MEPR I, Sterba intends (see ch2 note 2, 133) his MEPR I to apply only to those cases where the evils (the infliction of which would violate someone's rights) are not inflicted in order to provide some subsequent good (for the agent or some other rational being). He contrasts this with MEPR II and III, which apply to evils inflicted on someone in order to provide that human or some other rational being with some good. Given that, what MEPR I says is that everyone who can easily do so (without violating anyone's rights) should not permit immoral actions which have horrendous evil consequences when permitting these consequences does not make possible any good. Who could deny that?

I assume that, like MEPR I, MEPR III is governed by a clause such as 'so long as it can easily be done'. In that case what MEPR III says, is that everyone who can easily do so should not permit the occurrence of

EVILS ARE LOGICALLY COMPATIBLE WITH GOD'S EXISTENCE 43

immoral actions which have horrendous evil consequences, simply in order to provide someone with a good to which they do not have a right, and which could be provided in 'countless morally unobjectionable ways' without God needing to permit the evil. Again, that is obvious. Hence I am happy to endorse both MEPR I and MEPR III; but I shall be claiming that nothing God does violates these requirements.

But I cannot endorse MEPR II without qualification. Like the other requirements, it is a requirement not to permit certain sorts of immoral actions which would violate the rights of certain humans. Like MEPR III, it requires an agent not to do this in order to provide certain goods. But unlike MEPR III, it has no clause stating that it applies only 'when there are countless morally unobjectionable ways of providing those goods', and so it applies whether or not there is any morally unobjectionable way of providing those goods. It does, however, contain a complicated clause that an agent should not provide goods for someone if the goods are ones they 'would morally prefer not to have'. However, the clause that the goods should be ones which the recipient would 'morally' prefer not to have, adds nothing to the overall requirement. For in Sterba's sense of a 'moral preference' (defined ch2 note 7, 134) as one which it would be morally wrong not to have, any goods which could only be provided by a means which would violate the rights of recipients would clearly be goods which the recipients would be morally wrong not to prefer not to have. Because it adds nothing to the overall requirement, I shall in future ignore that clause.

I shall be claiming that God would sometimes be justified in permitting humans to do certain immoral actions with certain horrendous evil consequences, in order to provide certain goods, when those goods could not be provided in any way which did not involve God permitting horrendous evil consequences. Sterba, however, claims that MEPR II always applies, even if there is no way of providing the good without doing so in a way which involved permitting horrendous evil consequences. So that is the requirement crucial for our dispute. Here it matters greatly whether the 'rights' to which MEPR II applies are N-rights, which those humans have in all circumstances and which even God has no right to curtail. Sterba seems to imply (ch2, note 13, 134) that they are N-rights. If they are N-rights, then it seems to be an obvious tautology that it is always obligatory not to violate them; and I shall be claiming that God does not violate such rights. But if they are not N-rights, but G-rights, then God has the right to curtail, and so in that sense 'violate', those rights. So MEPR II applies to God only if the 'rights' which Sterba discusses are in fact N-rights, as he often implicitly assumes that they are. But, as I illustrated in section I, many often cited 'human rights' are P-rights or S-rights; and that it is plausible to suppose that they are in addition G-rights, as are also many other rights.

I shall be arguing that God does no wrong if he permits the horrendous evil consequences of certain immoral actions to be inflicted (by others or, in the case of God causing natural evils, by himself) on some rational beings,–when doing so would violate (in the sense of 'curtail') their S-rights and P-rights, if this is logically necessary in order to provide them or others with a comparable good.

In section I, I made the point that as God is so much greater a benefactor than our parents and the State, it is to be expected that he would have far more right to curtail human rights, and so cause us to suffer, than do parents and the State. I shall now illustrate by two examples, that parents have the right to permit their children to suffer significant (although not horrendous) evils caused by others, in order to provide those children with goods to which they do not have a right, when there is no way available to the parents with their limited powers of providing that good, other than one which causes a significant evil. If that is case, then it is to be expected that God, who is so much more our benefactor than are parents and State will have the right to impose on us much greater evils than they do for the sake of much greater goods; and begin to make it plausible that God has the right to permit horrendous evils in order to provide such goods, if it is not logically possible for him to provide those goods in any way which does not cause horrendous evil.

Here are my examples of situations where plausibly MEPR II, amended so that it concerns only 'significant evils' and not 'horrendous evils', does not apply, because the rights which they concern are P-rights which parents have the right to curtail for good reasons. In a previous version of his essay Sterba gave an example of a 'significant' evil which anyone who can easily prevent has—he considered—a duty to prevent.

This was the example of 'a small child...going hungry' and so, he presumably considered, not going hungry is a good to which the child has a right. Now suppose that I and my family are in a foreign country where there is a food shortage, although our family do have enough food so as not to hunger. I see some citizen of the country about to steal some of our food, in order to feed his family who have less food than we have and are hungry, although they are not starving. If I let the would-be thief steal the food, I and all my family including my 8-year-old daughter will go hungry, although she will not starve; but the thief's family will then not be hungry. I let the thief steal the food, explaining to my daughter that we, as a family, must be generous, supererogatorily generous, to help others in need (and especially others whose country it is); and thereby encourage the citizens of that country to show similar consideration for others in need. But in not preventing my daughter from going hungry, I have not violated anyone's rights. The thief has no right to our food, unless perhaps his family would otherwise starve: but that, I am supposing, is not the case; the thief is doing an immoral action. I am trying to teach my daughter that we must be supererogatorily generous in such circumstances; and insofar as she thereby begins to become a supererogatorily generous person, I help to provide her with a good to which she does not have a right. I reasonably believe that making her share in our family's common example of supererogatory love is at least as effective as any other method of helping her to become a supererogatory generous person. And, I suggest, I have the right to allow my daughter to go hungry in order to teach her that moral lesson; but since clearly no human other than a parent has that sort of right over my daughter, the daughter's right not to go hungry is only a P-right.

Here is a similar example. Suppose that I have a 16-year-old son who is a student at a 'tough' boarding school, and I learn that he is being bullied, which he hates. It is plausible to suppose that in all circumstances bullying is an immoral act, and a 'right' not to be bullied is, I suspect, one which Sterba would recognize. (It is plausibly a consequence of UDHR Article 5, which affirms that 'no one shall be subjected to...degrading treatment'.) I have the power to stop my son being bullied by withdrawing him from the school, and sending him to a different school where he will not be bullied. But knowing my son, I reasonably believe that he could stand up for himself in the face of this bullying, and I encourage him to do this, believing that he will emerge from the experience as a stronger and more self-confident person. I also point out to him that if he does stand up to the bullies, that will have the further good of encouraging others also to stand up to them. Thereby I cause my son to suffer a significant evil, but believe correctly that there is no more readily available means of achieving the good of him becoming a more self-confident person. I suggest that as a parent, I have the moral right to determine which school he should attend (UDHR Article 26); and I suggest that in these circumstances I do not have an obligation to withdraw him from the school. It follows that the right not to be bullied is not a N-right but only a P-right.

Note two crucial features of my examples. The first feature is that the right to permit the evils involved belongs to parents, and to no other human authority. No human other than a parent has the right to permit a child to go hungry or to be bullied, if they can easily prevent this. The second feature is that the parents do what they do for the sake of the moral character of the child, and in part also for the sake of the moral character of others. If parents whose responsibility for the existence, nurture, and security of their children is very limited, have very limited rights of the kind described, it becomes highly plausible to suppose that God whose responsibility for the existence of humans lasts as long as they exist and is so much greater than that of a parent, has the right to impose much greater evil on humans for the sake of the moral well-being of the sufferer and of other humans. This is especially the case since God is perfectly free and perfectly well-informed, and knows the effects of his actions in influencing humans far better than do parents. I believe that the State also has the right to permit the occurrence of significant evil consequences of immoral actions to be inflicted on its citizens in order to provide them with goods; but—for reasons of space—I do not develop such an example here.

What I shall be claiming with respect to all the evils, whether horrendous or merely significant, which—if there is a God—he permits to occur, is that by doing so, God makes possible a comparable good; and it is not logically possible that God can provide that comparable good in any way which does not involve the occurrence of a similar evil. To take the most obvious example of a significant (though not horrendous) evil where this is the case—if God is to give us the great good (and one to which we do not have a right) of being allowed free choices of whether or not to help people in trouble, there must be people in trouble. There is no other way—let alone 'countless other ways'—in which God could give us this serious free choice without the possibility of unprevented-by-God evil suffered by others. And I shall be arguing that the good is a comparable good, and so God is justified in allowing the evil to occur.

Sterba's first three 'natural evil prevention requirements' have more or less the same form as his three 'moral evil prevention requirements'. All humans, he claims, have a right not to suffer horrendous natural evils; and so, if some humans are able to prevent these evils, they have an obligation to do so; and, if humans cannot or will not prevent them, God has an obligation to prevent them. However, I have argued that many so-called 'rights' are only P-rights or S-rights, and since God is so much more our benefactor (as well as so much wiser) than are parents or the State, God has far greater right to curtail supposed human 'rights' than they do. Hence it is to be expected that God (who can do anything logically possible) has the right to permit many natural evils, so long as doing so is logically necessary for some comparable good.

My general conclusion at this stage of the argument is that Sterba cannot simply affirm that there are a lot of obvious human 'rights' which are such that even God has no right to permit the occurrence of evils which violate them. Sterba needs to argue with respect to particular actual evils, that those particular evils are ones which even God has no right to permit, or that they do not make possible any comparable good. He has not even attempted to do this.

III. Human Goods and Their Accompanying Necessary Evils

In this section I seek to show that for almost all known evils, moral and natural, only if God permits these and so causes or helps to cause them, would he be able to provide for us many of the very great goods which we enjoy on earth; and I shall argue that these are comparable goods. I shall approach this issue by listing the great goods which many of us enjoy on earth, and which—if there is a God—God provides for us; and I shall then analyse for which of them God would have to have permitted the occurrence of which evils.

It is good to have pleasurable sensations, and good health, to eat well and live in a comfortable house in a good environment; and to be able to enjoy some of the innumerable harmless pleasures which so many humans enjoy, such as singing, dancing, running, playing football or chess, watching TV; and also learning important truths about the world. And it is better if we are in these situations and do all these actions jointly with other people. God could provide all this for us without permitting any evils to occur.

But a good life contains more and greater goods. It is very important for our well-being that we depend on others, and others depend on us; that is, we are supported by others, and we support others. In particular, it is very important that the good things necessary for our well-being, such as those listed above, are provided for us by parents who are responsible for us during the early part of our lives and freely choose to exercise that responsibility in a loving way which is good for us, however difficult that is for them to do. And it is equally important for most of us that as adults we have a spouse and children for whom we are responsible during a significant part of their lives, and freely choose to exercise that responsibility in a loving way which is good for them, however difficult that is for us to do. But our parents can only be truly responsible for us if they have sometimes the free choice of whether to benefit or harm us in significant ways. If they were programmed so as only to benefit us and not harm us, their choices of how to show love would not be nearly so valuable. We want a care which comes, not by the chance operation of some impersonal force or some unknown manipulator which causes our parents to act, but by their free choice. And our children rightly want the same sort of care from us. And even if, as is normal and good, we and our parents both have a natural desire to show love, most of us have competing desires, short-term or long-term, and are tempted to pursue them too often at the expense of our children. We show our love in these circumstances by freely choosing to resist the competing desires. Most humans become parents; and so, however poor and ill educated they are, have the enormous responsibility of caring for their own children; they have awesome choices of either taking considerable trouble to make their children happy, showing them how to live, and helping them to grow in so many ways; or of neglecting to do so. It is a great good for all of us that we can choose to show love when it is difficult but needed, and an even greater good if in fact we choose to do so.

It is another great good if we are able freely to influence humans other than our children in good or bad ways; and almost all humans have considerable opportunities to influence at least some other humans for good or bad. And again it is an even greater good for us, if we use these opportunities to make the good choices, and thereby improve the world, and so become an ultimate source of significant good in the world. Under God our Creator, we would be 'mini-creators'. This great good is the good, not merely of being able to make choices which God permits to cause their intended effect only if they are good choices, but the great good of being able to make choices that cause their intended effect, whether good or bad; and of course it is a further great good if we cause the good effect.

These free choices, if they are to be free in a significant way, need to result from the exercise of libertarian free will, as defined earlier. I believe that humans do have libertarian free will, but this is a matter of enormous philosophical and scientific controversy, which it is not possible even to begin to discuss in a small book devoted primarily to a different topic. So, as this is how it seems to most of us as we make our choices (and as we implicitly assumed in the Introduction to this book), I shall assume that we have some limited free will of this kind.[7] In that case, as we noted in the Introduction, it is not logically possible for an omnipotent God to give us the freedom to choose between good and evil, and yet cause us to choose the good. If God gives us this choice, he thereby permits the possibility of us causing much moral evil; and so, given the large number of humans and the large number of free choices they make, it is very probable that there will be much moral evil in the world.

Our free will is clearly limited by the alternative actions which it even occurs to us that we might do, our beliefs about the effects of our actions and our inadequate moral beliefs about what is morally good or bad, and also by the desires which influence (although do not fully determine) us to make the choices which we make. To have a moral choice between doing a morally good action or doing a morally bad action (which may be just the action of not doing the morally good action) we must be subject to some desire to do the bad action. This is because a belief that some action is morally good to do, motivates us to do the action. I could not believe that some action was really morally good to do, and yet not see myself as having a reason for doing it; and I could not see myself as having a reason for doing it unless I had some inclination (= desire) to do it; and the better I believe some good action to be, the greater will be my inclination to do it. So in order to have the choice of doing either a good action or a bad action, we must be subject also to some bad desire (= temptation) inclining us to do the bad action. Then we will have the free choice of which desire to yield to and which desire to inhibit; without the bad desire we would automatically do the good action. As a result of our genes and upbringing, we find ourselves with certain desires which we may be able to change in the course of time; but at any particular time we are stuck with the desires which we have. The bad desires are natural evils, necessary if we are to have the great good of being able to choose freely between morally good and morally bad actions. Yet the relative strengths of the good and bad desires, which make some choices easier than others, put a further limitation on the freedom of our free choice.

It is good that most of us do not too often have very many desires deliberately to hurt other humans—humans would be nasty people if we did. Hence we can only have the opportunity to make important moral choices and so deep responsibility for others (and ourselves), if the normal alternative to doing good to others is negligence—doing nothing, when doing nothing involves allowing others to suffer as a result of natural processes. Hence the need for the natural evils of suffering caused by disease, accident, and old age.

Most natural evils cannot readily be cured or alleviated; and so, just as when they are the victims of a morally evil choice, humans suffer, often for considerable periods of time. But such suffering provides significant opportunities for crucial choices, both for the sufferer and for their family, friends, and wider society. Others have the choice of whether to console the sufferer and try to cure the suffering or to ignore the sufferer;

and the sufferer has the choice of whether to bear their suffering with patience and cheerfulness or to allow themselves to become bitter about it. It is especially good that sometimes we should have the opportunity to show courage over a long period in the face of serious suffering, and thereby show great commitment to the good. And it is especially good that sometimes we should be able to help those who are seriously ill or deprived, for providing help at their time of greatest need is an act of deep significance.

As well as being able to make a difference to other humans, it is a further enormous good for us that by doing so, we form our own character, determine what sort of person we are to be. Our character is a matter of the kinds of desires and beliefs and their strengths which we have—whether we are naturally generous, kind, considerate, friendly, and well-informed about the needs of others and so about which actions of ours would have what kind of influence on them, and whether we care about the nature of reality, including about the existence of God. Or whether we are naturally selfish, angry, envious, and callous and without adequate understanding of the needs of other humans and without any ambition to understand reality. Humans are so made that making choices on each occasion to do a good action of some kind strengthens our desire to do a similar good action in future, and making choices to do a bad action of some kind strengthens our desire to do a similar bad action in future. We can thus gradually change our desires, so that we naturally desire to help others, and are not merely driven to do so by a nagging conscience. In order that we should have the choice of forming a strong very good character, we need to have opportunities (occasionally) to do actions which involve resisting great temptations (strong bad desires), because thereby we manifest our total commitment to the good and put us on the way to being by nature very good people. Or alas by repressing the nagging conscience, we may allow ourselves to become very bad people—God allows us to reject his ideal for us.

It is good for us that we should form our characters over a considerable period of time by choosing whether to investigate what makes for moral goodness, or not to bother, combined with many opportunities to make choices between what we discover to be good and bad actions. This ensures that our choice of a good character was one thoroughly thought and worked through. And it is manifestly a good for us if we cannot come to have a bad character by a quick spontaneous action, but only by allowing ourselves to make many bad choices over a considerable time, despite our consciences continually prodding us to do the opposite.

It is good too that among the choices available to humans should be the choice, not merely of whether or not to help others to cope with natural evils such as diseases which afflict them personally, but of whether or not to try to reduce the number of such natural evils in future, and so prevent future diseases. But to have this choice we need to know what causes these evils. The normal way in which we (and in today's world that often means the scientists among us, supported by money from the rest of us) try to discover such things is the inductive way. That is, we seek to discover the natural processes (bacteria, viruses, etc.) which bring about diseases, and then construct and further test theories of the mechanisms involved. But scientists can only do that if there are regular processes producing the diseases, and they can only learn what these are by studying many populations and studying under which circumstances some disease is transmitted and under which circumstances it is not transmitted. So for the great good of this choice of investigating (or, alternatively, not bothering to investigate), there is required the necessary evil of the actual disease. God could have caused us all to be born with the knowledge of how to cure diseases, but he has given us the great gift of rationality, and it is very good that we should be able to exercise it (or choose not to bother to exercise it) by working this out for ourselves. But if humans are to have the great opportunity of devoting their lives to scientific research to cure actual evils such as disease, there have to be humans suffering from disease; and hence an additional good, provided by the natural evil of the suffering.

Another reason why it is good that the human race should sometimes be in an initial situation of considerable ignorance about the causes and effects of our actions, is this. If God abolished the need for rational inquiry and gave us from childhood strong true beliefs about the causes of things, that would make it too easy for us to make moral decisions. As things are in the actual world, most moral decisions are decisions taken in uncertainty about the consequences of our actions. I do not know for certain that if I smoke, I will get cancer; or that if I do not give money to some charity, people will starve. So we have to make our moral decisions on the basis of how probable it is that our actions will have various outcomes—how probable it is that I will get cancer if I continue to smoke (when I would not otherwise get cancer), or that someone will starve if I do not give. Since probabilities are so hard to assess, it is all too easy to persuade yourself that it is worth taking the chance that no harm will result from the less demanding decision (the decision which you have a strong desire to make). And even if you face up to a correct assessment of the probabilities, true dedication to the good is shown by doing the act which, although it is probably the best action, may have no good consequences at all.

It is not only freely chosen morally good intentional actions of various kinds which involve reactions to natural evils, which constitute a good for their agents; but morally good actions performed involuntarily also do so, although these constitute a lesser good for those who do them. If prisoners were compelled to clean sewers, they would surely be right to regard that as a good for them in comparison with being useless, because they were contributing to the well-being of the community. There is also a further benefit for the sufferer, which lessens the evil of their suffering, if their suffering provides the opportunity for others to do morally good actions additional to helping the sufferer. 'Being of use to others' by what we suffer involuntarily is often a significant benefit for the person who is of use. Consider someone badly injured in an accident, where the accident leads to some reform which prevents the occurrence of similar accidents in the future—for example, someone injured in a rail crash which leads to the installation of a new system of railway signalling which prevents similar accidents in the future. The victim and his relatives often comment in such a situation that at any rate he or she did not suffer in vain. Although they still rightly regard the suffering as on balance an evil, they would have regarded it as a greater misfortune for the victim (quite apart from the consequences for others) if his or her suffering served no useful purpose.

It follows from one being-of-use to someone else, either by what one does (voluntarily or involuntarily), or by what happens to one, that two humans are benefited thereby. Whenever God allows some natural evil to occur to B, and in particular causes B to suffer, in order to provide some good for A (for example, the free choice of how to react to this suffering) that B is benefited as well—B's life is not wasted, she is of use (by enduring the evil). She is of use to A, but she is also of use to God; she plays a role in God's plan for A. And to be of use to the good source of being in the redemption of his creation is an enormous good.

So the starving, the persecuted, and the abused are of use to those who live comfortable lives and have no natural interest in the lives of others, because—but for the former forcing the latter to pay attention to them, the latter would have no opportunity to be of any great use to anyone—their lives would be so self-centred as to be largely worthless. The starving, the persecuted, and the abused are the vehicle whereby alone the comfortable and self-obsessed can have a serious free choice of whether to be saved from self-obsession and learn to give their time and money and energy to helping others. And thereby they are of use to God himself.

I can well understand that it might be a natural reaction of many readers at this stage of the argument, to feel that I fail to take seriously the horrors of starvation, persecution, and abuse. I hope that I am not failing in this respect. But I am taking very seriously how important it is that humans should live lives of use to others by what they do and by what they are; and by forcing themselves to do so and by encouraging others to force themselves to do so, come to desire to do so; and that is worth a great price to achieve. I am also relying on my assumption that the lives on earth of the vast majority of humans are on balance good lives. That may not be initially apparent in the case of many who suffer. But we need to bear in mind that in their suffering, sufferers often have the deep love of parents and children, and fellow-sufferers, and that makes their own struggles such that on balance, their lives are still worth living. I argued earlier that it is reasonable to assume that God will provide for those to whom my assumption does not apply, an afterlife, the goodness of which outweighs the evil of their earthly life.

It will, I suspect, also be a natural reaction of many readers to feel that the suffering which is necessary for the goods which I describe, is divided very unevenly. Some have significant free choices which make great differences to others, but do not suffer much themselves; and while many suffer much from disease and other natural evils, others suffer very little from natural evils. So it is natural for the sufferers to feel that the distribution of evils is not 'fair'. But given the earlier assumption that for the vast majority of humans life on earth is on balance good, God does these sufferers no wrong. God, like a good parent, gives different assignments to different children, thereby acknowledging their individuality and their need to play a particular role in the scheme of salvation. To be allowed to suffer for a good cause is a privilege, even if the only good brought about by the suffering is that the sufferer has made themself a saint—not bitter at their suffering, not bitter when others neglect them, always cheerful and always concerned for the well-being of others. That good is an enormous good—for the sufferer, as well as for others. The apostles flogged on the orders of the Jewish Sanhedrin 'rejoiced that they were considered worthy to suffer dishonour the sake of the name [of Jesus]' (Acts of the Apostles 5:47).

But, having made these points, I nevertheless recognize that the benefit to some human of doing a good action involuntarily or of 'being of use' by what they suffer is normally not as great a good as the evil which they suffer is an evil, and so our benefactor God must take that into account when he ensures that our life overall is on balance a good one.

In this section I have described many good features of our lives which make them good to live, but which necessarily involve the probability unprevented-by-God of many moral evils and the actual occurrence of many natural evils. Every moral evil is such that God allowing its agent the free choice of causing it (or not preventing it), or, alternatively, not causing it (or not preventing it) is a good for that agent. And, the harder it is to make the good choice, the greater the value of the choice if it is made—the child of dishonest parents who forces himself not to lie to save himself from being convicted of theft has done an act of deeper significance than the child of honest parents who does not have to try so hard to tell the truth in similar circumstances. Virtually every natural evil is such that the sufferer has the free choice of whether to react to it well or badly (unless the sufferer is too young or mentally disabled to be able to make that choice—in which case those who have the moral responsibility for caring for the sufferer have that choice). All free choices in the face of moral or natural evil are character-forming. But it is also the case that most of these evils provide some good for someone else as well as the sufferer, as when someone's suffering provides an opportunity for others to react to it in ~~the~~ right ways, and to develop medical treatments to avoid it in future. These evils provide the framework for the exercise of human love for each other when it is most needed and most valued.

I hope that, by my description of the various good states made possible by the various evils, I have begun to make it plausible that each evil state is such that causing or helping to cause it makes possible various goods which together constitute a comparable good. But if an opponent still claims that the typical moral evils of society, such as rape, and cruelty to children, are so awful that there could not be any comparable good made possible by allowing them to occur, I draw attention to the following further consideration. Each of these evils is such that the State could take very strong action which would largely or entirely prevent their occurrence; but this would inevitably involve the elimination of some good which the State wishes to maintain, and almost all liberal minded citizens will agree that it should not take that very strong action. Thus the State could prevent cruelty to children by removing children immediately after birth away from their natural parents and educating them in a home staffed entirely by caring foster parents. But very few liberal minded citizens would support this measure. The State could very largely prevent rape by the powerful deterrent of installing CCTV in every room in every house and on every corner of every street, and having these CCTVs continually watched by police who would immediately arrest any rapist, and get them imprisoned for many years. But again very few liberal minded citizens would support this measure. These two examples show that liberal minded citizens think that there are comparable goods which would be eliminated if the State took sufficiently stringent measures to prevent rape and cruelty to children—the goods of biological parents (however imperfect) bringing up their own children (the right to which seems to be implied by UDHR Article 16), and the good of privacy in our personal lives (the right to which is explicitly stated in UDHR Article 12). Hence (if we share the intuitions of liberal citizens) what this shows is that the evils are not so abhorrent that no one would ever be justified in allowing them to occur; a State would be justified in allowing them to occur if it would not be possible for it to prevent them except by eliminating these good states.

It follows that if the good states which would be eliminated by any action of God that could prevent these evils, are as good as the good states which would be eliminated by the actions which I have described, then the good states which would be eliminated by any action of God are comparable good states. God can do anything logically possible; and so, unlike the State, he could eliminate these evils in some way other than the ways which I discussed. But it would not be logically possible for God to eliminate the possibility of rape without eliminating either strong sexual desires or our free will to choose whether or not to yield to desires as strong as these; and those, I suggest, are great goods. Strong sexual desires are central to the very good institution of marriage; and the good of us having the choice of whether or not to yield to strong desires just is the good of libertarian free will. God could eliminate cruelty to children in some way other than by taking them away from their natural parents; but it would not be logically possible for him to eliminate it without eliminating either the free will of parents to treat their children either well or badly, or the responsibility of parents for the upbringing of their own children, which is such a good thing for the parents, and also normally (despite its obvious bad aspects) for the children. I suggest that it is in no way obvious that the goods which would necessarily be eliminated if God eliminated the possibility of rape and cruelty to children are inferior to the goods which would be eliminated by the State if the State took the measures which I described. Hence there is no justification for the view that these social evils are such that any good God ought to have prevented the possibility of their occurrence. I suggest that a similar dialectic would show a similar conclusion with respect to other widespread social evils, that by allowing the evils to occur God makes possible the occurrence of comparable goods.

I am not of course suggesting that the State should not take strong measures to reduce the occurrence of rape and cruelty to children and similar evils, but I am pointing out that there are limits to the measures which the State ought to take to secure these ends. The State should try to secure these ends primarily by education and persuasion, by funding social services which, together with neighbours, will help those in trouble.

Considerations similar to those which apply to social moral evils, apply to widespread natural evils, such as pandemics. I am writing this at the height of the Covid pandemic when there is vigorous discussion about the measures which should be taken to prevent its spread. The strongest measures to prevent its spread would be to confine everyone to their houses except for a few chosen workers who would produce and deliver the minimum amount of food necessary to keep people alive. But the normal view of liberal minded citizens is that that would be going too far. It would eliminate crucial goods—for example, the good of economic prosperity and the social interaction needed for mental health and the education of children. So implicitly the State recognizes that there is some maximum proportion of citizens who should be allowed to become seriously ill and die from Covid in order to preserve such other goods. God could eliminate all pandemics without eliminating the goods of economic prosperity and social interaction. But again, as I pointed out earlier, God could not eliminate diseases without eliminating great opportunities for the sufferer and others freely to cope with their suffering and make themselves very good people, and to use their reason and their energy and money to make a healthier world.

We saw in section I that God has the right to impose evils on some human only if God remains on balance that human's benefactor (GBC I); and I have now argued that if we also insist that God has the right to impose an evil only if that evil is a logically necessary condition for some comparable good state (GBC II), that that condition is also normally satisfied for humans who suffer significant evils on earth.

I have conceded that there is a small minority of humans whose openness to suffering benefits others, but whose own lives on earth are on balance not worth living. My argument has the consequence that God has an obligation to compensate these humans for the evil they suffer in this life by a good afterlife, so that the total life of such people will be on balance good; and that, I have argued, in virtue of his perfect goodness, he will do. This point is crucially relevant to the case of babies abused by their parents, who die before they can get any pleasure out of life at all. It is still the case that their life is of great value, because by their openness to such abuse, they provided their parents with the choice either of abusing them or not abusing them; and so by their availability to suffering, they made available a great good for the parents, which alas the parents misused. Also, what has happened to the baby often becomes known and so leads to measures in the community to avoid such abuse in future. But the earthly lives of these babies were clearly not on balance such that it was good that they had lived them. Hence God must, and according to most Christian thinkers will, provide a far better life for them after death.

IV. Horrendous Earthly Evils and Glorious Heavenly Goods

I have argued so far that for most kinds of evils, there are comparable goods which they make possible; and so God our Creator is totally morally justified in allowing them to occur to humans, so long as each human life is on balance (on earth, or in a few cases after earth) a good one. But the issue still remains whether there are some evils so horrendous that they never make possible a comparable good. Sterba acknowledges that God should allow humans to do immoral actions with 'significant' consequences, but he denies that it would ever be morally right for God to permit immoral actions with 'horrendous' consequences. The difference between 'significant' and 'horrendous' evils is a matter of degree. There is no sharp line between them; but clearly some evils are a lot more horrendous than others. The issue at stake is whether some evils are so horrendous that God would never be justified in allowing them to occur for the sake of any resulting good.

It seems to me obvious that Sterba's suggested world in which no evil was worse than the evil of a boy being terrorized for several hours would indeed be a moral kindergarten, a 'toy world' in which our choices would matter, but they wouldn't matter enormously. A world where the worst choices we could make were of the degree of evil similar to that of the boy being terrorized for several hours would not be a world where God has entrusted humans with choices which have profound effects on themselves and other humans.

It may be suggested that the occurrence of a significant evil in a large number of humans, for example in a pandemic or as a result of a deliberate policy of killing a whole population, constitutes an evil so horrendous that God would never be justified in allowing it to occur. But surely if God has the right to permit any one individual human to suffer in the Covid pandemic for many months in order to provide the opportunity for significant choices both to the sufferer and to their friends of how to deal with this suffering, then God has the right to permit many humans to suffer at the same time in order to provide significant choices for each of them and their friends. In fact, if a large number of people suffer simultaneously, that normally produces considerable compassion and help from the wider population who are not directly affected by themselves or their loved ones suffering, and serious action by States to help and prevent such pandemics in future. The mere number of sufferers cannot affect the cogency of a justification of God allowing some evil.

But are there any kinds of actual evils, such that the suffering of one human of any instance of that kind is so horrendous that God would never be justified in permitting it to occur, whatever the comparable good which it makes possible? Death is not such an evil; it is the end of a good state—life. But only God, as the giver of life, has the right to take it away from someone (except in certain of the circumstances where killing some would save the lives of others, as in a just war). God takes away most human lives by natural biological processes. Although this often causes much sadness for relatives and friends, without the seriousness of death, as I pointed out earlier, so many of our actions would be without deep significance.

What is much more worrying is when the horrendous character of an evil consists in the great suffering of one or more individual humans, in a long and painful illness, or—the most horrendous evils of all—by cruel torture of a kind to which a considerable number of people have been subjected by sadists and by political and religious zealots in the course of human history. A proper initial reaction to some accounts of what humans have done to other humans can only be to weep. It is important, however, to bear in mind that there is always a limit to the amount any human can suffer in their earthly life, and that means at most a hundred years or so; and that is a very short time in comparison with the time after death in which God, if he so chooses, can give to sufferers a very good life, the goodness of which will outweigh the badness of their suffering. And anyone subjected to intense torture for more than a few days is likely to die at that stage. Death is God's safety barrier. I am not claiming that there is no possible evil that God would not be justified in allowing us to suffer, and so I am not denying that we have some N-rights, rights which even God does not have the right to curtail. I am merely claiming that God has the right to allow us to suffer the actual evils of this world. So the issue between Sterba and myself is a quantitative one—the amount of suffering by any one human, which a perfectly good God is justified in permitting.

So what comparable goods are made possible by God ever permitting evils such as the horrendous evils of torture or of suffering from some very painful disease to be endured by anyone? I suggest that in permitting these evils, God is allowing two kinds of human a final choice of what sort of being they are to be, what character they will have for ever in future. First, God is allowing the very good to become saints. I have been arguing that it is good for God to allow humans important choices between doing good and yielding to some bad desire, both for their own sake and because of the effects which our choices have on forming our character. Good parents want their children to live good lives; and will encourage them to do so by word and example, and sometimes—as I argued in section II—put them in a position where they have an opportunity to make a choice of how to react to an unpleasant situation. But clearly there is a narrow limit to the unpleasant situations that a mere human parent would be justified in imposing on a human child.

However, a perfectly good God, being so much more the author of our existence than are our parents, and so much more knowledgeable about the effects of actions than are humans, and able to compensate sufferers for any suffering they would endure, would rightly be very ambitious for the humans whom he has created. He would not be content with humans being moderately good people enjoying a fairly worthwhile life. He would want us to be saints. I mean by 'a saint', a person who has a resolute overriding desire not to yield to lesser desires to do what is morally bad, is totally committed to doing actions exhibiting great love for others and for truth, and—because he or she has such a strong desire to do such actions—enjoys doing such actions, above all if they are successful in making others happy and good, and propagating true views. God would want all of us to be saints, but might prefer not to force sanctity on us against our will; and so he might want to give us the free choice of making ourselves saints. If we make the good choices very often, we shall become good people; but we may still be subject to bad desires and there may be a limit to our willingness to resist them. It may need a final choice of doing the good action under very difficult circumstances in order finally to cement our commitment to the good.

'Greater love has no human than this, than to lay down their life for their friends' (John 15:13) said Jesus. He laid down his life by allowing himself to be crucified. A similar love may be shown in many different ways, both by religious persons and by non-religious persons, for example, allowing themselves to be tortured without revealing the whereabouts of their friends whom tyrannous authorities wish to kill, or refusing to deny a belief which seems to them to have enormous importance for the world. Or their sanctity may be shown by bearing the suffering of some terrible disease with patience and cheerfulness.

If someone does make that ultimate commitment to the good in the face of severe suffering, it follows from the principle which I enunciated earlier that God must provide for every human a life which is on balance a good life, that he must provide for those suffering such severe suffering a compensatory life after death. But for those who freely make that ultimate commitment, a good God would surely think them worthy of an endless life where they could have perfect free will to choose between innumerable good alternatives, but would at last be spared having any bad desires and so any pains or other suffering necessary on earth for them to choose what sort of person they are to be. There would be no need for suffering in heaven. It would therefore be very good if humans have finally chosen the good, that they should continue to do for ever after death the good actions which make a life on earth good, in an ever deeper way—including understanding ever more about God and worshipping him ever better, growing in ability to understand everything else, and helping more and more other people (including people still on this earth or other earths) to be in this situation and to do these actions. According to the Christian Bible and later patristic tradition, the Blessed in heaven are in this situation and do these actions, being finally free from suffering and temptation.[8] Only those whose desires are solely to live in this way would be permanently happy in heaven; others who still have nagging self-centred desires would not be eternally happy living that life.

This last point provides part of the answer to an often made objection that, if a life in heaven is really a very good life to live, as of course Christianity and other theistic religions claim that it is, then surely it would be better for God to put everyone in heaven to begin with. It is, however, very good for humans to have the choice of the sort of character they will have, and so the choice of whether or not to live the life of heaven. The other part of the answer to the objection, is that humans need other humans to suffer in order to provide that choice for them, by giving them the opportunity to react to our actual and possible suffering in the right way. We have this opportunity on earth.

The great value of an ultimate total commitment to the good explains the Christian reverence for the martyrs who made that ultimate commitment by allowing themselves to be killed by some very nasty process rather than denying their faith, and the Christian confidence that they are now in heaven. And of course it is a further good for a saint that, by allowing themselves to be killed in a very painful way, they give great encouragement to others to live better lives. Throughout human history the lives of saints have been of enormous importance in encouraging the rest of us to begin to travel the road to sanctity.

But also, by permitting the occurrence of horrendous evils, God allows very bad humans to become totally evil. A perfectly good God would want to give us a final choice about the sort of character we will have (the sort of person we are to be), and so God would permit us totally and finally to reject goodness itself, to reject everything that he stands for. Clearly he would not permit this without allowing us many different opportunities to halt our downward slide. But if he did not allow us finally to reject him, he would not give us the ultimate free choice. It is good that a rejected suitor should try many times to persuade a beloved one to accept a proposal of marriage, but it is not good that a rejected suitor should try an endless number of times to secure this result—it constitutes a failure to recognize the beloved as someone who has the right to decide their own future. Even God, I suggest, should be willing in the end to take no for an answer.

If that is correct, then there will be a final occasion when an evil human by doing a very evil act, finally eliminates the nagging of conscience, and so loses any concept of moral goodness. This final act, and those immediately preceding it, would involve choosing between doing or not doing some very evil act, and so involve the possible occurrence of a horrendous evil. That choice would not be available in a 'toy world'; it is only if someone has no qualms about causing a horrendous evil for no good reason and are glad to do it, that they have finally manifested their rejection of the good. But, when faced with that choice, ordinary evil people may finally face up to the horror of evil, and by making at last a good choice (at least by repenting what they are doing, and so becoming committed to trying to avoid doing any such action in future), rather than the very evil choice (of doing it without regret), begin a climb back from the abyss. But of course if any humans make very evil choices, others will suffer horrendously. Those others will, however, but not through their own choice, be in a position to bear their suffering in such a way that they can choose to make themselves saints.

In his chapter on the Soviet police interrogators in *The Gulag Archipelago*, Alexander Solzhenitsyn commented on the awful possible final effects of very evil choices:

> Evil has a threshold magnitude. Yes, a human being hesitates and bobs back and forth between good and evil all his life... But just so long as the threshold of evildoing is not crossed, the possibility of returning remains, and he himself is still within the reach of our hope. But when, through the density of evil actions, the result either of their extreme degree or of the absoluteness of his power, he suddenly crosses that threshold, he has left humanity behind, and without, perhaps, the possibility of return.[9]

Solzhenitsyn seems to suggest that some of the Soviet KGB interrogators whom he encountered had crossed that threshold.

By contrast Simon Wiesenthal in his book *The Sunflower*, tells us about one SS man who was content to obey orders to treat people of occupied Poland in various cruel ways until he was commanded to set light to a house into which many Jews had been crowded. He obeyed the command; but, as he heard the screams of the burning Jews, he did not suppress his horror at what he was doing and was moved to a deep genuine repentance, and so began a journey on the road to sanctity.[10] But these choices would not have been open to the KGB interrogators or the SS soldiers without the possibility of horrendous evils.

It would be good that God should give us a free choice while on earth about whether or not to aspire to the life of heaven. But we can only do that freely in a world where there is great opportunity for total self-sacrifice. This is not the place to discuss at length how God might deal with people who die in an intermediate condition, as most of us probably do, of having some dedication to the good, and some considerable weakness of will as a result of which we sometimes do what is evil. As a result of weakness of will, some humans will collapse morally under their horrendous or lesser suffering: but, insofar as they make some attempt to cope with it, God will surely compensate them for their suffering in the next life. Others of us are moderately good or bad people, who have never had opportunity to make big serious choices. God might put those who die in any intermediate condition into a situation in the next world where they had to make big serious choices; or he might make the good choice for them, and give to those who have not in any way rejected the good that total dedication to the good which they have not fully chosen for themselves. Catholic Christianity, with its doctrine of Purgatory, holds that many of us have still to purge ourselves from our sinful character before we are admitted to heaven; and Orthodox Christianity seems to allow for the possibility that our eventual destiny is not always permanently settled at our earthly death. But my point is that it is a great good for us if our future depends on our own free choices; and if some people are to have the great good of it depending on them, as well as by their example providing a uniquely great stimulus for ordinary people to live better lives, then horrendous evils which they choose willingly to endure out of love for God and other humans, ensure that people have that choice.

Sterba may claim that the price of us having such choices is too high. I have argued that it is perfectly compatible with God's perfect goodness to create such a world, and he violates no obligations to his creatures by creating one. Sterba would need to show that my moral intuitions on the relative goodness and evil of different lives and states of affairs are false, before he could claim with any justification to have a *deductive* argument from 'objective moral truths discoverable by rational reflection' (to quote our Introduction) for his view that the world's actual evils are logically incompatible with the existence of God. I suggest that not merely has Sterba failed to do this, but also that he has failed to recognize the enormous value of sanctity; and that a perfectly good God might well provide every encouragement to each of us freely to choose to do those actions which will make us saints.

4
Response to Swinburne

James Sterba

I begin my response to Richard Swinburne's essay by first briefly restating my argument that the God of traditional theism is logically incompatible with all the evil in the world. I then respond to Swinburne's specific objections to that argument. After which, I turn to a consideration of Swinburne's own argument in defence of the God of traditional theism and show that given Swinburne's own normative premises, the God of traditional theism is logically incompatible with all the evil in the world.

I. My Argument

My argument[1] begins with a fourfold classification of all the goods that God could provide to us:

(1) Goods to which we have a right that are not logically dependent on God's permission of especially horrendous evil consequences of immoral actions.
(2) Goods to which we have a right that are logically dependent on God's permission of especially horrendous evil consequences of immoral actions.
(3) Goods to which we do not have a right that are not logically dependent on God's permission of especially horrendous evil consequences of immoral actions.
(4) Goods to which we do not have a right that are logically dependent on God's permission of especially horrendous evil consequences of immoral actions.

I then set out three necessary moral requirements. These requirements are exceptionless minimal components of the Pauline Principle never to do evil that good may come of it, which would be acceptable to consequentialists and nonconsequentialists alike. These requirements would be acceptable to consequentialists and nonconsequentialists because as these minimal components of the Pauline Principle have been formulated, there are no good consequentialist or nonconsequentialist reasons for violating them. Theists and atheists should also accept these requirements for the same reasons that consequentialists and nonconsequentialists accept them. Here they are:

Moral Evil Prevention Requirement I
Prevent rather than permit especially horrendous evil consequences of immoral actions without violating anyone's rights (a good to which we have a right) when that can easily be done.

Moral Evil Prevention Requirement II
Do not permit rather than prevent the infliction of especially horrendous evil consequences of immoral actions on their would-be victims in order to provide would-be beneficiaries with goods they would morally prefer not to have.

Moral Evil Prevention Requirement III
Do not permit rather than prevent especially horrendous evil consequences of immoral actions (which would violate someone's rights) in order to provide would-be recipients with goods to which they do not have a right that are not logically dependent on God's permission of those consequences when there are countless morally unobjectionable ways of providing those goods.

Then I apply these three requirements (MEPR I–III) to my fourfold classification of goods and get the following results:

1. MEPR I prohibits God's provision of goods of type (1) by his permitting especially horrendous consequences of immoral actions. With respect to goods of type (1), we are sometimes stuck in a situation where we can only provide some people with

such a good and hence prevent a corresponding evil from being inflicted on them by not providing other people with another good whose non-provision inflicts a lesser evil on them. For example, we may only be able to save five people from being robbed and viciously assaulted who are close by if we don't try to also save two other people from being robbed and assaulted who are farther away. God, however, would never find himself causally stuck in such situations. God would always have the causal power to prevent both evils. Accordingly, God would have to prevent both evil consequences in all such cases, as needed, unless there is a good that either does or does not logically presuppose the existence of some serious wrongdoing which would justify God in permitting the lesser evil in such cases.

2. MEPR II eliminates any need for goods of types (2) and (4) by requiring God's prevention of especially horrendous consequences of immoral actions. With respect to goods of type (2), like the good of needed medical aid after one has been brutally assaulted, or goods of type (4), like the good of having the opportunity to provide needed medical care after someone has been brutally assaulted, given such goods depend on the existence of horrendous moral wrongdoing, it would be morally required for anyone who could do so without violating anyone's rights to prevent the consequences of that wrongdoing on which those goods depend.

Hence, the would-be beneficiaries of such goods would have morally preferred that anyone who could have done so without violating anyone's rights would have prevented the consequences of the wrongdoing on which those goods depend. For example, a victim of a vicious assault and the person who would care for him both would have morally preferred that anyone who could have done so without violating anyone's rights would have prevented the consequences of the assault to their now having the goods that are logically dependent on those consequences.

3. MEPR III prohibits God's provision of goods of type (3) by permitting especially horrendous consequences of immoral actions. With respect to goods of type (3), both God and ourselves would have numerous ways of providing people with such goods without

violating anyone's rights by permitting rather than preventing especially horrendous evil consequences of immoral actions to be inflicted on them. In cases where we humans are causally constrained by lack of resources and are thus unable to provide someone with such a good without permitting the horrendous violation of the person's rights, God would never be subject to such causal constraints.

Still, it might be objected that while it may seem appropriate, even required, for God not to permit rather than prevent especially horrendous evil consequences of immoral actions in any particular case, once we generalize that behaviour for all such cases, morally objectionable consequences result. Thus, suppose that you had done all that you could to prevent the consequences of some horrendously evil action and you could see that you were not going to be completely successful. Suppose that at that moment God were to intervene and provide what is additionally needed to completely prevent all the evil consequences of that action. Presumably, you would be pleased that God had so intervened. Now imagine you are again considering whether to intervene to prevent the consequences of another horrendously evil action. You might reason that if you did intervene you might well be successful this time. Yet upon further reflection you might decide that there is really no need for you to intervene at all because if you do nothing, you could now assume that God would intervene as he had done before, and this time completely prevent the evil consequences from happening. So you do nothing.

Here, I claim, God would be morally required to intervene to prevent the evil consequences of that action, but in this instance, God's prevention should only be partially successful. Here is why. Originally, let's say, you were in a position to prevent the abduction of a small boy into a car. Now that you have chosen to do nothing, you witness the abductors successfully driving off with the boy. Only later do you learn that the car was subsequently stopped many miles away by a passing patrol car because it had a busted tail-light, and the small boy, whom the kidnappers had terrorized and were planned to kill was then discovered in the car and freed by the police. So, you assume, not unreasonably, that God was involved in this prevention as well as in the earlier one. Nevertheless, you cannot help but note that the intervention was not as successful as it presumably would have been if you had chosen to intervene yourself. After all, imagine that you were standing close to the boy. You could have just screamed to alert others and/or pulled the boy away and completed foiled the abductors. As a result, the boy would not have been terrorized as he was during the time he was in the hands of his abductors before the police were able to rescue him.

So, in this hypothetical world, you begin to detect a pattern in God's interventions. When you choose to intervene to prevent especially horrendously evil consequences, either you will be completely successful in preventing those consequences or your intervention will fall short. When the latter is going to happen, God does something to make the prevention completely successful. Likewise, when you choose not to intervene to prevent such consequences, God again intervenes but not in a way that is fully successful. Here there is a residue of evil consequences that the victim still does suffer. This residue is not a horrendous evil, but it is a significant one, and it is something for which you are primarily responsible. You could have prevented those consequences, but you chose not to do so and that makes you responsible for them. Of course, God too could prevent those harmful consequences from happening even if you don't. It is just that in such cases God chooses not to intervene so as to completely prevent both the significant as well as the horrendous evil consequences of wrongful actions in order to leave you with an ample opportunity for soul-making. One might argue, as I would, that the God of traditional theism should prevent both the significant and the horrendous consequences of immoral actions in such contexts, but if God were to prevent just the horrendous evil consequences of such actions that would clearly make the world much, much better than the world we currently inhabit, and it definitely would not turn the world into a moral kindergarten since we would be able to prevent both the significant and the horrendous consequences of immoral actions, sometimes with God's help when we chose to do so, and when we chose not to do so, we would be responsible for the significant evil consequences of those actions which we are imagining God chooses not to prevent in this case to give us an ample opportunity for soul-making. Instead of being a moral kindergarten, it would be a world that morally good people would prefer to inhabit. It is just not our world in which the horrendous evil consequences of immoral actions abound, consequences that an all-good, all-powerful God of traditional theism, if he existed, would not have permitted.[2]

Now Swinburne objects to the above argument claiming:

> A world where the worst choices we could make were of the degree of evil similar to that of the boy being terrorized for several hours would not be a world where God has entrusted humans with choices which have profound effects on themselves and other humans. (Chapter 3, p. 59)

But what would we think of Swinburne's claim if it were transformed into the following:

> A political state where the worst choices citizens could make were of the degree of evil similar to that of the boy being terrorized for several hours would not be a political state which has entrusted its citizens with choices which have profound effects on themselves and other citizens.

Now I don't think that our reaction to this transformed claim would be that the political state has failed to entrust its citizens with enough choices but rather it would be that it had already entrusted its citizens with too many.

Just imagine a police officer seeing a group of hoodlums terrorizing a young boy and walking by and doing nothing to stop them. Clearly, we would find that unacceptable behaviour on the part of the officer. Now imagine a case where the hoodlums were planning to torture to death a young boy and again the police officer seeing what was going to happen did not intervene when he could easily have done so. In that case, would we object to God causing a severe rainstorm that disrupted the hoodlums allowing the boy to make his escape? I think we would have welcomed God's intervention as a last resort in all such cases.

Still, Swinburne could agree with me that it follows from his view that a political state which ensured that the worst choices its citizens could make were comparable to the evil that obtained in my example of the young boy 'would not be a political state which has entrusted its citizens with choices which have profound effects on themselves and other citizens'. But then he could counter that on his view no political state has the right to impose on its citizens the profound choices involved in allowing boys to be tortured for several hours, let alone permit other horrible evils. This is because the political state, being a lesser benefactor than God has very limited rights to impose evils upon us for whatever good purpose. Instead, Swinburne would argue that God, as our supreme benefactor, has the right to impose very serious choices on us which would give us the opportunity to make great differences to our own character and to the well-being of others. Swinburne calls this the opportunity to become saints by our own free choice.

It is just here, however, that a fundamental conflict arises. It turns out that if political states are successful at doing what they ought to be doing, that is, successful at establishing states in which their citizens all have an equal freedom for soul-making then no way would be left open for God to permit unequal freedom as well. Hence, no one would have the opportunity to impose horrendous evil consequences on others, and so, in Swinburne's terms, no one would have the opportunity to be a saint—the ultimate good that God, as supreme benefactor, was supposed to be providing us.

Yet this shouldn't happen. There should be a way, under ideal conditions, for political states to be successful at doing what they are supposed to be doing at the same time that God could also be successful at doing what he is supposed to be doing. Unfortunately, that cannot obtain under Swinburne's account because fundamental moral requirements are at odds in his account.

Nor would it help to imagine God starting us off with the unequal freedom necessary for having an 'opportunity to be saints' because then we could easily imagine political states being successful at doing what they ought to be doing thereby transforming that unequal freedom that God initially provided into an equal freedom for soul-making for all its citizens. Hence, the conflict persists between the just political state's goals and what Swinburne takes to be God's goal for us.

What is very important to realize here is that no such conflict obtains for my account. Accordingly, if political states successfully achieve what they are aiming to achieve and provide everyone with an equal opportunity for soul-making by preventing all horrendous evil consequences from being inflicted on their would-be victims, as needed, God, on my account would still have a bona fide role to play. God would still be the preventer of last resort for the system of equal liberty for soul-making that the political state seeks to maintain, and God would in no way be at odds with the political state if it is successful in securing an equal liberty for all its citizens, since that is God's goal as well. Hence, there is a fundamental conflict in Swinburne's account between a political state's morality and God's morality that undermines his account, a conflict not found in my account.

II. Swinburne on MEPR I–III

It is important to recognize that Swinburne accepts MEPR I and MEPR III as exceptionless moral requirements that are binding on both God and ourselves. In his terminology, they are N-rights, rights that even God logically cannot violate.[3] This means the whole debate between Swinburne and myself comes down to the status of MEPR II. If MEPR II, like MEPR I and MEPR III, is an exceptionless moral requirement, an N-right, then Swinburne would have to accept my conclusion that the God of traditional theism is logically incompatible with all the horrendous evil consequences of immoral actions in the world. This is because, on Swinburne's account, all the horrendous evil consequences of immoral actions in our world result from what would have to be justified exceptions to MEPR II. Accordingly, if there are no morally justified exceptions to MEPR II, if it is an exceptionless moral requirement like Swinburne recognizes MEPR I and MEPR III to be, then, for Swinburne, like myself, it is not logically possible for the God of traditional theism to exist given all the evil in the world.

So how then does Swinburne purport to show that MEPR II is not an exceptionless minimal moral requirement? Let's start with the requirement:

Moral Evil Prevention Requirement II
Do not permit rather than prevent especially horrendous evil consequences of immoral actions on their would-be victims in order to provide would-be beneficiaries with goods they would morally prefer not to have.

Now Swinburne contends that the clause 'that they would morally prefer not to have' in the requirement itself along with its further specification in the text 'adds nothing to the overall requirement'. This means that for Swinburne MEPR II with the clause about moral preferences and its further specification in the text has no more content than the requirement without that clause and without its further specification in the text. Whereas for me, this clause of MEPR II with its further specification in the text adds sufficient content to the requirement to transform it into an exceptionless moral requirement like MEPR II or MEPR III.

Here it is clearly relevant that Swinburne acknowledged in correspondence between us that a similar transformation occurred for him with respect to MEPR I. As it so happened, it was not until Swinburne took into account the further specification of MEPR I found in the text that he came to recognize MEPR I as an exceptionless moral requirement. Could then the further specification of MEPR II in the text similarly require Swinburne to recognize MEPR II as an exceptionless moral requirement?

In my further specification of MEPR II in the text, I argue that it would be conclusively morally wrong for the beneficiaries not to have the required preference given that they can have the greatest good of the opportunity to be friends with God, the resources for a decent life, as well as many other opportunities for soul-making, without availing themselves of those goods on which God's permission of horrendous evil consequences depend.[4] Hence, I claim, the would-be beneficiaries would conclusively morally prefer not to be implicated in the violation of people's fundamental rights that would obtain if they were to utilize such goods given that they don't otherwise need and can easily do without them while still enjoying the opportunity to be friends with God, the resources for a decent life, as well as many other opportunities for soul-making. This then is the kind of moral preference that, I claim, would-be beneficiaries would have under MEPR II. It is a moral preference that it would be conclusively morally wrong for them not to have because it expresses an exceptionless moral requirement just like MEPR I and MEPR III.

Here it is important to note the similarity of MEPR II to MEPR I. Let us begin with MEPR I:

> Prevent rather than permit the infliction of especially horrendous evil consequences of immoral actions without violating anyone's rights (a good to which we have a right) when that can easily be done given that for this requirement there are no competing goods at stake.

Now for MEPR I, preventing especially horrendous evil consequences is conclusively required given that it can be easily done and given that there are no competing goods at stake. Yet although for MEPR II there are competing goods, those goods are not only morally objectionable by being logically dependent on horrendous evil consequences but also they are not otherwise needed because their would-be beneficiaries can have the greatest good of the opportunity to be friends with God, the resources for a decent life, as well as many other opportunities for soul-making, without availing themselves of those goods on which God's permission of horrendous evil consequences would depend. So, those morally objectionable goods can easily be done without. Hence, in their different but similar ways, MEPR I and MEPR II both express conclusive/exceptionless moral requirements.

Here it is also important to note the similarity of MEPR II to MEPR III. Let us begin with MEPR III:

> Do not permit rather than prevent especially horrendous evil consequences of immoral actions (which would violate someone's rights) in order to provide would-be recipients with goods to which they do not have a right that are not logically dependent on God's permission of those consequences when there are countless morally unobjectionable ways of providing those goods.

In the case of MEPR III, the goods that God would otherwise be permitting horrendous evil consequences to provide could be provided in countless morally unobjectionable ways, and hence, they should be provided in those morally unobjectionable ways. Whereas for MEPR II, the goods that God's permission of horrendous evil consequences would make possible are not otherwise needed and can be easily done without, and therefore, should not be provided in this morally objectionable way through God's permission of horrendous evil consequences given the availability of other goods, including the greatest good of the opportunity to be friends with God, the resources for a decent life, as well as many other opportunities for soul-making, that can be provided without God's permission of such horrendous evil consequences. Hence, in their different but similar ways, MEPR III and MEPR II both also express conclusive/exceptionless moral requirements.

To better see how MEPR II is a conclusive/exceptionless moral requirement, consider the following analogy. Imagine that a very rich person could become a few dollars richer if a poor person is wrongfully deprived of all she has. These few dollars wrongfully taken from the poor person are clearly something the rich person does not need and can easily do without. Consequently, it is a no brainer that the rich person should conclusively morally prefer that God prevent rather than permit the poor person's being wrongfully deprived of all she has for the benefit of the rich person.

Now the analogy to the standard case for the application of MEPR II should be clear. The rich person is analogous to the would-be beneficiaries of the goods made possible by God's permission of horrendous evil consequences because they too are 'rich' since they can have the greatest good of the opportunity to be friends with God, the resources for a decent life, as well as many other opportunities for soul-making, without receiving any goods on which God's permission of horrendous evil consequences depend.

Correspondingly, the few dollars wrongfully taken from the poor person are analogous to the benefits from soul-making that the would-be beneficiaries don't really need and can easily do without because again they can have the greatest good of the opportunity to be friends with God, the resources for a decent life, as well as many other opportunities for soul-making, none of which depend on God's permission of horrendous evil consequences of immoral actions being inflicted on innocent victims. Hence, just as the rich person should conclusively morally prefer that he not be benefited at the cost of wrongfully depriving a poor person of all she has, so too the would-be beneficiaries of the infliction of horrendous evil consequences should conclusively morally prefer not to be provided with goods that the infliction of those horrendous consequences on innocent victims makes possible.

Now I contend that it is only because Swinburne failed to take into account the further specification of MEPR II in the text that he failed to recognize the similarities between all three MEPRs and so failed to recognize that not only MEPR I and MEPR III, but also MEPR II is an conclusive/exceptionless moral requirement, or in Swinburne's terminology, that it is an N-right, a right that even God could not be violating.

Still, Swinburne does attempt to undercut MEPR II as a *conclusive/exceptionless* moral requirement by offering two counterexamples against it.

Here is a version of his first counterexample:

> Suppose that I and my family including my 8-year-old daughter are in a foreign country where there is a food shortage, although our family has enough food and so are not hungry. I see some citizen of the country about to steal some of our food to feed his family who have less food than we have and are hungry, although they are not starving. Suppose I do not prevent the thief from stealing the food, explaining to my daughter that we, as a family, must be supererogatorily generous, to provide a good for others in need. So, despite the fact that she prefers me not to do so, I provide her with the good of having the opportunity willingly to associate herself with our family's generosity and its hoped-for consequences.

And here is a version of Swinburne's second counterexample:

> Suppose that I have a 16-year-old son who is a student at a 'tough' boarding school, and I learn that he is being bullied, which he hates. I have the power to stop my son being bullied by withdrawing him from the school and sending him to a different school where he will not be bullied. But knowing my son, I believe that he could stand up for

himself in the face of this bullying, and I encourage him to do this, reasonably believing that he will emerge from the experience as a stronger and more self-confident person; and believing correctly that there is no less unpleasant way of achieving this aim. However, my son would prefer me to move him to a different school, where he will not be bullied. This preference [Swinburne thinks] is a moral preference, because the son has no obligation to be bullied.

In both of these examples, the daughter and the son respectively, would have all things considered reasons to override their initial preferences not to act as their father directed them to do. Accordingly, these cases might serve as counterexamples to MEPR II if that requirement had been formulated in terms of significant evil consequences.[5] Nevertheless, the requirement is not formulated in terms of significant evil consequences but in terms of the horrendous evil consequences of immoral actions, and that difference is essential to what makes them conclusive/exceptionless moral requirements. Given then that MEPR II, like MEPR I and MEPR III, applies only to cases that would involve the permission of horrendous evil consequences of immoral actions, Swinburne's 'counterexamples', applying as they do to just significant evil consequences, have no bearing on the justification for MEPR II as I have formulated it. Moreover, what Swinburne's 'counterexamples' show is that the permission of significant evil consequences can be morally justified in our world, typically for soul-making, and this accords well with my own argument which maintains that the God of traditional theism, if he exists, could be justified in permitting significant, but not the horrendous, evil consequences that obtain throughout our world. Moreover, justified permitting of significant evil consequences, as in Swinburne's 'counterexamples' does not even 'indirectly' support justified permitting of horrendous evil consequences, especially for paradigm cases of structural evils, like the Holocaust, where my exceptionless moral requirements MEPR I–III clearly apply and forbid God's permitting horrendous evil consequences.

In sum, Swinburne has endorsed my MEPR I and MEPR III as exceptionless moral requirements. However, with respect to MEPR II, he has failed to take into the account the further specification of that requirement I provide in the text and so has failed to come to terms with my argument that MEPR II is a conclusive/exceptionless moral requirement just like he recognizes both MEPR I and MEPR III to be. Moreover, his counterexamples are perfectly consistent with my view, and so in no way oppose it.

Now Swinburne does maintain that the God of traditional theism being a super-benefactor has the right to permit horrendous consequences of immoral actions in order to provide us with goods that could not be provided in any other way as long as there is a moral justification for doing so, which in Swinburne's terminology means there is a comparable good. Unfortunately, Swinburne fails to take into account my argument contained in the further specification of MEPR II for why there is no such moral justification for doing so, *therefore*, no comparable good. Hence, any God that exists who is lacking a justification for permitting all the horrendous evil consequences that obtain in our world could not be our benefactor, let alone our super-benefactor.

III. More on My Argument

Now it is important to recognize the overall form my argument against the God of traditional theism takes. In our Introduction, Swinburne and I claimed:

> Arguments between theists and atheists usually begin with the assumption that the all-good, all-powerful God of traditional theism exists. Atheists grant this assumption for the sake of argument, and then go on to claim that it is inconsistent with the existence of evil. Theists usually think they have some independent argument for the existence of that God. Both theists and atheists believe that evil exists, where evil is understood to be either moral evil or natural evil.
>
> Beyond the assumption that the all-good, all-powerful God of traditional theism exists and that evil exists without which there would be no problem of evil, the crucial question is what additional premises are to be added to complete the argument. Either there are additional

premises about what is morally required or permitted that can be added to these two assumptions that show the compatibility of the God of traditional theism and all the evil in the world, or there are additional premises about what is morally required or permitted that can be added to these two assumptions that show the incompatibility of the God of traditional theism and all the evil in the world. Which is it? That is what this debate between the two of us (Sterba and Swinburne) is all about.

For the sake of argument, I have also been willing to grant Swinburne and other theists the assumption of libertarian freedom, even though I think that a compatibilist account of freedom is more defensible. In addition, given that a connection of the permission of evil in the world to a heavenly afterlife is almost always endorsed by theists, I have been willing to grant Swinburne and other theists the assumption of a heavenly afterlife as well. In return, Swinburne and other theists have granted, or better just simply acknowledged, the indisputable fact that the God of traditional theism, if he exists, would be permitting all the horrendous evil consequences of immoral actions that occur in the world. Thus, in the argument between atheists and theists, atheists, like myself, are willing to grant theists, for the sake of argument, a lot of useful assumptions, asking only in return that theists grant the existence of all the horrendous evil consequences of immoral actions that exist in the world, something that would be difficult for theists to deny even if they had wanted to do so.

I can also restate my argument to approximate what John Mackie should have used to succeed in his famous exchange with Alvin Plantinga as follows:

(1) There is an all-good, all-powerful God. (This is assumed for the sake of argument by both Mackie and Plantinga.)
(2) If there is an all-good, all-powerful God, then necessarily he would be adhering to Moral Evil Prevention Requirements I–III.
(3) If God were adhering to Moral Evil Prevention Requirements I–III, then necessarily especially horrendous evil consequences of immoral actions would not be obtaining through what would have to be his permission.

(4) Especially horrendous evil consequences of immoral actions do obtain all around us, which, if God exists, would have to be through his permission. (This is assumed by both Mackie and Plantinga.)
(5) Therefore, it is not the case that there is an all-good, all-powerful God, which contradicts (1).

Now the whole focus of my argument is to show that when my three necessary moral requirements (MEPR I–III) are applied to the goods with which God could provide us (which include the prevention of evils), they require that the God of traditional theism, if he exists, prevent the especially horrendous evil consequences of immoral actions, which he clearly has not done. To show this, I see no need to provide either a general theory of rights or a list of some of the widely recognized prima facie moral rights that people have endorsed. I see my argument as compatible with many such theories of rights and many lists of prima facie moral rights, including Swinburne's own.

Swinburne too appears to recognize that this is the focus of my argument. That is why he devotes the second section of his essay to trying to undermine my MEPRs with counterexamples. Fortunately, for my God argument, I have been able to show that Swinburne's counterexamples are not even directed at my argument.

IV. Swinburne's Argument

In his defence of traditional theism, Swinburne puts forth two normative conditions that he claims must be met in order for the God of traditional theism to be a perfectly good benefactor as he must be if he is the God of traditional theism. He calls them Good Benefactor Conditions (GBCs).

GBC I is that God must remain on balance a benefactor during the lives of those he creates. This means, Swinburne tells us, that at a minimum no one's life as a whole, which includes an afterlife, is such that one would be better off if one had never existed, except through one's own choices.[6]

GBC II is that God only causes, or helps to cause, an evil state if it is not logically possible that he can cause a comparable good state in any other morally permissible way.

At first glance, it might appear that GBC I is fairly straightforward. Surely, we can roughly assess when lives are going well or badly, and roughly determine when someone's life is not worth living. However, in developing his account, Swinburne introduces the idea of 'a good of being of use' as something that could count toward the goodness of a person's life, even when it is involuntarily imposed on the person. For example, think of a Black student who has been transferred into a predominantly white high school and is having difficulty dealing with the underlying racial hostility and microaggressions that she is experiencing at the new school. Suppose the student wants to be transferred back to her old predominantly Black high school where she would not face the same discrimination. Imagine that her parents and the school administrators refuse her request believing that this student, and others like her, can make an important contribution toward lessening the racial bias that happens to exist at the new school in which she is now enrolled. Hence, I think that this is a case where it is good for the student to be of use by contributing to the educational and moral development of her fellow students, even though she might initially be unwilling to do so. Yet, there are other cases where introducing the idea of 'a good of being of use' is not morally defensible as something that could count toward the goodness of one's life when it is involuntarily imposed. We will consider a case of this sort later.

Frequently, Swinburne refers to the standard guaranteed by GBC I as providing a 'good life' or 'on balance a good life'. To me, these expressions suggest a higher standard of well-being than is guaranteed by his official standard that no one would be better off if one had never existed, except through one's own choices. Accordingly, I will be interpreting Swinburne to be uniformly embracing the lower standard and rejecting the higher standard that he sometimes seems to be entertaining by claiming that people are assured of a 'good life' or of an 'on balance a good life'. There is also a good reason to interpret Swinburne's view in just this way. Only Swinburne's low standard could conceivably have been met by many of those who throughout human history have suffered from horrendous evil consequences being inflicted on them, such as those who just barely survived in Nazi concentration camps.

Initially, I thought that Swinburne's GBC I–II differed from MEPR I–III by only applying to God, but now (from correspondence) I see that Swinburne understands them to have the same applicability to benefactors as do my requirements, although Swinburne assumes that only God, if he exists, has a prima facie right to impose horrendously evil consequences on us while meeting GBC I. Still, Swinburne allows that this prima facie right can only become a conclusive right if GBC II is also satisfied.

Swinburne's GBC II tells us that God only causes or helps to cause an evil state if it is not logically possible that he can cause a comparable good state in any other morally permissible way. What then is this comparable good state that is logically related to God's causing or helping to cause the evil, which can include the horrendous evil consequences of immoral actions? For Swinburne, there is no mystery here. It is libertarian free choice, or let's say libertarian freedom, or just freedom and what is logically dependent on it.

a. More Freedoms at Issue

Yet here we have a problem. By freely choosing to impose the horrendously morally evil consequences of their actions on their victims the perpetrators of those actions also drastically restrict the freedom *to act* of their victims.

Now Swinburne does not usually describe what happens to the victims of horrendous evil as a loss of freedom *to act*.[7] Usually, he considers what happens to victims of horrendous evil as being harmed. But we can also describe the harm that is imposed on the victims of horrendous evil as a loss of freedom because it is that as well as being a harm. Moreover, by describing the harm as a loss of freedom, we can better compare what is gained by the perpetrators of horrendous evil actions against what is lost by the victims of those actions because we would be describing both what is gained and what is lost in terms of freedom.

We can also clearly see that the freedoms at stake do not have the same moral value. The freedom of would-be perpetrators not to be interfered with when inflicting horrendous evil consequences on their victims is a freedom that the perpetrators should not be exercising whereas the freedom of victims *to act without having* horrendous evil consequences of immoral actions inflicted on them is, by contrast, a freedom that would-be victims should be able to exercise.

Unfortunately, Swinburne fails to view conflicts between perpetrators and victims of horrendous evil consequences as conflicts of freedom because he fails to consider that if God exists, there would be a number of stages to God's bestowing of freedom on us. Instead, Swinburne understands God's bestowing of freedom to take place all at once, and so he never considers how God, if he exists, could, and in fact should, take a different stance toward the earlier stages of free actions than he takes to the final stage of free actions where horrendous evil consequences are inflicted on their victims by their perpetrators. The compelling reason for taking a different stance with respect to the earlier and later stages of horrendously evil actions is that only the final stage of such actions really takes away the significant freedom of the victims of the horrendous evil. The earlier stages, although of moral significance, are clearly not as important as the final stage for preserving the significant freedoms of the would-be victims of horrendous evil.[8]

Notice too that assessing differently the stages of free actions is something we ourselves do through our political institutions. For example, notice that those of us with bad thoughts and intentions who for various reasons never go on to threaten or take significant steps to impose bad consequences on others, do not, on that account, make it into the criminal justice systems of the political states to which we belong. This is because our political institutions are focused on preventing and deterring that final stage of immoral actions, the stage that takes away the significant freedoms of would-be victims, thus punishing only those who are found guilty of inflicting, or who were about ready to inflict such bad consequences on others. Hence, just as we morally expect an ideally just and powerful political state to prevent, where possible, the final stage of especially horrendous evil actions, so likewise, should we morally expect the all-good, all-powerful God of traditional theism to prevent the final stage of especially horrendous evil actions, as needed. Yet we know that this has not happened. Hence, any God that exists by failing to prevent the final stage of especially horrendous evil actions as required by Swinburne's own freedom requirement, correctly interpreted, as well as by my MEPR I–III, would not be our benefactor, let alone our super-benefactor as required by Swinburne's GBC I. As Swinburne himself says in a related context, 'help is most significant when it is most needed and it is most needed when the recipient is suffering and deprived'.[9] And this is just when God, if he exists, would be leaving much horrendous suffering and deprivation unmet, and hence, by Swinburne's own implied standard, God, if he exists, would not be our benefactor, helping us when we are most in need, let alone our super-benefactor.

b. The Different Stages of Free Actions Employed in MEPR I–III

In formulating my Moral Evil Prevention Requirements (MEPR I–III), I focused on whether there would be a justification for God's not preventing, hence permitting, the final stage of especially horrendous evil actions of wrongdoers, the stage where the wrongdoers would be imposing those evil consequences on their victims. I assumed that there would be a justification, at least in terms of freedom, for God's not interfering with the imaginings, intending, and even the taking of initial steps by wrongdoers toward bringing about such consequences on their would-be victims. I also assumed that there could be a justification, at least in terms of freedom, for God's not interfering when the consequences of immoral actions are not horrendously evil. Moreover, theists would also have to assume the same, given that if a God exists, he is, by and large, not demonstrably intervening in these domains of our lives. Hence, it would have to be that God, who is assumed to exist, also endorses the same justification for noninterference with respect to the consequences of immoral actions which are not horrendously evil that I claim an ideally just and powerful state would endorse. What this does is divide our acts of free choice into earlier stages and its final stage where especially horrendous evil consequences are being imposed on the victims of those actions. Hence, it is only to that final stage of our free actions that my MEPRs apply.

You can also see this failure of Swinburne to take into account the different stages of our free actions in his commentary on our claim in the Introduction that 'it is not logical possible for an omnipotent God to give us the freedom to choose between good and evil and yet cause us to choose the good'. Here too Swinburne sees God giving us freedom in an all-at-once bestowal and not something that could be provided at one stage while not provided it at another, just the way a political state might allow serious wrongdoers the freedom to imagine, intend, and even take some initial steps to carry out their horrendous wrongdoing, but still deny them the final freedom to inflict horrendous evil consequences on their victims, when they have a justifiable way of so denying them. Clearly, the ability to provide a morally differentiated response to the different stages of free actions is widespread in human affairs. Hence, this ability must also be available, par excellence, to the God of traditional theism, if he exists.

Swinburne's defence of God's permission of the horrendous evil consequences of immoral actions, therefore, turns on regarding the free action that God permits to be an all-in-one bestowal whose value is assessed before the action has begun when the expected value of its final stage is quite different from the expected value that stage will have just before the infliction of horrendous evil consequences on would-be victims. Thus, it is only when imposing horrendous evil consequences becomes the almost inevitable consequence of the perpetrator's action that God's permitting that final stage of the perpetrator's action becomes completely outweighed by the loss of significant freedom that the action is about to impose on its victims. Hence, Swinburne's freedom defence for God's permission of horrendous evil consequences of immoral action does not succeed because it fails to distinguish between the different stages of free actions and to see the need for God to respond to them differently, specifically by permitting the earlier stages of especially horrendous evil actions while preventing the final stage of those actions just when their horrendous evil consequences are about to be imposed on innocent victims.

c. Rejected by Both Perpetrators and Beneficiaries

Yet not only do the freedoms of the victims who have horrendous evil consequences of immoral actions imposed on them completely outweigh the freedoms of the perpetuators to impose those evil consequences, but, in addition, the perpetrators themselves, if they ever morally repented their wrongful deeds, would for all eternity morally prefer that their freedom had been restricted by God's prevention of just the horrendous evil consequences of their actions. Those perpetrators who repented would recognize that their freedom to inflict those horrendous consequences should never have been exercised. Rather, their victims should have been able to exercise their far more morally important freedoms. Moreover, even those who would have acted virtuously, and hence, benefited morally when faced with the opportunity to do great good or great evil would also for all eternity morally prefer that their freedom and the corresponding freedom of others to do great evil had been similarly restricted to their having an unrestricted opportunity to do good and evil. They would only be content if an equal freedom to do good and evil were effectively secured for all, such as did not obtain with respect to Joseph Mengele and his experimental human subjects at Auschwitz.

d. A Choice That Is Not Universalizable

Beyond its failure to be morally justified, there is still a further problem with Swinburne's idea that God wants to provide us all with the option to do great good and great evil. It is that this option cannot even be provided to *all* of us. We cannot all jointly exercise this freedom together unless virtually every one of us opts to do what is morally good. This is because as soon as some of us choose to do especially horrendous evil actions, the imposition of the consequences of those actions will preclude others from having the same freedom that the perpetrators exercised. Hence, the freedom Swinburne says God wants all of us to have cannot be enjoyed by all of us as long as some of us wrongfully choose to impose horrendous evil consequences on others and are not prevented from doing so.

e. More Virtuous

Nor is having the option to do great good and great evil needed for the exercise of high virtue.[10] In fact, constraining one's own freedom as well as the freedom of others to do evil is what is required to be more virtuous. To see this, compare the capacity for being virtuous of wealthy individuals acting alone to meet the needs of the starving, possibly in a state of nature, to the capacity of the same individuals for being virtuous when they are constrained and empowered through a political state's requirement that all its members fairly contribute to meeting the needs of the starving. Political states are thus used to collect resources, both from those who would otherwise be willing and from those who would otherwise be unwilling, to fairly contribute to meeting the needs of the starving. Accordingly, wealthy individuals who willingly act through such political states would, other things being equal, be more effective at meeting the needs of the starving than those who just act alone to do so as in a state of nature. Hence, these individuals would turn out, other things being equal, to be more virtuous in this regard as well.[11]

It is also important to see here that meeting the needs of the starving is just one way of preventing at least significant, and most likely, horrendous evil consequences of immoral actions. Hence, the above argument can be generalized to maintain that our obligation to prevent especially horrendous evil consequences of immoral actions similarly requires that we both constrain and empower ourselves through the political state to which we belong to prevent such consequences. Thus, we should constrain ourselves in this way from imposing such consequences on others, even when we would not do so if we acted independently. In this way, we would be able to more effectively, and hence, other things being equal, more virtuously discharge our obligation to prevent horrendously evil consequences from being imposed on others than we would be able to do by just acting alone as in a state of nature. Swinburne agrees with this, but then he is at pains to point out that acting unconstrained can be virtuous too. Now while there is no denying that is the case, the point being made here is simply that when good and bad people act together under the constraints of an ideally just political state with God acting as the constrainer of last resort, they can be more virtuous, especially because they are more capable of producing just outcomes, than when acting independently of such constraints.

Of course, our willingness to constrain ourselves in accordance with the requirements of a political state to more effectively produce just outcomes should depend on the political state actually doing what it is supposed to be doing. Consequently, checking to make sure that this is actually occurring is also a requirement of virtue in this context.

It should also be acknowledged that in our world, good people who would otherwise want to live in an ideally just and powerful state may still be reluctant to give the existing states that they inhabit the power to prevent all the especially horrendous consequences of immoral actions, even if the advanced technology for doing so were available. This is because good people could reasonably be worried that if state officials ever had the power to prevent especially all the horrendous evil consequences of immoral actions, they would be tempted to use that power to act immorally instead. Nevertheless, while this problem does arise with respect to human administrators of just and powerful states, there is no comparable problem when God is understood to be the constrainer of last resort because God, if he exists, would be morally incorruptible. It is this morally incorruptible God of traditional theism who should be the constrainer or supporter of last resort for existing just political states, and when such states do not yet exist, such a God should be the instigator and catalyst for the formation of such states, as needed. Moreover, morally good administrators of just and powerful political states would not find it problematic, in fact, they would welcome the intervention of the God of traditional theism as the constrainer of last resort.

Still, it might be objected that if God were ever to start acting as preventer of last resort of horrendous evil consequences, good people would no longer have the motivation to prevent such evil consequences themselves. Now I faced this same objection earlier when I restated my argument against the existence of the God of traditional theism at beginning of this essay. There I argued that when we choose to intervene to prevent especially horrendously evil consequences of immoral actions, either we will be completely successful in preventing those consequences or our intervention will fall short. When the latter is going to happen, I claim, God should do something to make the prevention completely successful. Likewise, when we choose not to intervene to prevent such consequences, I claim, God should again intervene but not in a way that is fully successful. Here there is a residue of evil consequences that the victim still does suffer. This residue is not a horrendous evil, but it is a significant one, and it is something for which we are primarily responsible. We could have prevented those consequences, but we chose not to do so and that makes us responsible for them. Of course, God too could prevent those harmful consequences from happening even if we don't. It is just that in such cases, God should choose not to intervene so as to completely prevent both the significant as well as the horrendous evil consequences of wrongful actions in order to leave us with an ample opportunity for soul-making. I argued that if God were to prevent just the horrendous evil consequences of such actions in this way, it would clearly make the world much, much better than the world we currently inhabit, and it definitely would not turn the world into a moral kindergarten since we would be able to prevent both the significant and the horrendous consequences of immoral actions, sometimes with God's help, when we chose to do so, and when we chose not to do so, we would be responsible for the significant evil consequences of those actions which we are imagining God would choose not to prevent in such cases in order to give us an ample opportunity for soul-making. Instead of being a moral kindergarten, it would be a world that morally good people would prefer to inhabit. It would just not be our world in which the horrendous evil consequences of immoral actions abound, consequences that an all-good, all-powerful God of traditional theism, if he existed, would not have permitted.

To see how God's intervention is needed even when it would result in his revealing his presence to us, consider the following example. Imagine a teenager is violently assaulting a much younger sibling while two other siblings close in age to the younger sibling look on in wide-eyed astonishment. Imagine that just then the parents show up, stop the assault, and severely condemn and punish the teenager. Now consider how the children who just witnessed the assault are to evaluate what occurred. Do they judge the abuse morally wrong in itself or is their condemnation of the assault significantly influenced by their parents' actual condemnation and punishment of it?

Suppose the latter is the case. Would this mean that the parents should not have intervened so that these children could have more easily made an independent moral evaluation of the assault? Clearly, we do not think that this is what the parents should do. Whatever concern the parents have for helping their children understand the intrinsic wrongness of immoral actions, that does not override their own moral responsibility to prevent serious and especially horrendous evil consequences of their children's actions when that is required.

The same considerations apply to just and powerful political states in their dealings with serious wrongdoers on those occasions when the state's dealings with the wrongdoers happen to be witnessed by bystanders. There too the state's response to such wrongdoing can have an impact upon the moral evaluations of the bystanders that may complicate their moral assessment of the wrongdoing. Nevertheless, whatever concerns a political state would have in helping its citizens understand the intrinsic wrongness of serious immoral actions, those concerns would not override the state's moral responsibility to prevent serious and especially horrendous evil consequences of those actions when that is required.

Accordingly, analogous considerations obtain with respect to God and our moral assessment of especially horrendous evil actions. Whatever concern that God, if he exists, would have with regard to helping us understand the intrinsic wrongness of horrendous evil actions, it would not override his responsibility to prevent the consequences of those actions when that is needed.

f. Natural Evils

No one disputes that we need to know the effects of natural evils in order to know how harmful they are, and when they are horrendously harmful, we need to know how to avoid them. But we don't generally need to acquire this knowledge ourselves by direct experience and experimentation with those evils, as Swinburne seems to suggest.[12] Much of that knowledge can be passed on to us from others, and they themselves may have acquired it from still others.

There are also at least two general reasons why we frequently do not want to acquire such knowledge ourselves either by direct experience or experimentation. First, it would be good if each of us could avoid, so to speak, inventing the wheel again by wasting our time and resources discovering things that others have already discovered and could just pass on to us. Second, it may be extremely dangerous for us to try to acquire certain kinds of knowledge by direct experience or experimentation.

Of course, our parents, teachers, and others just more experienced than ourselves are aware of the learning process that we all go through in our lives, and if all goes well, those around us will help us acquire the previously secured knowledge we need, and new knowledge as efficiently and as safely as possible. Moreover, many of those who guide us through this learning process will function as important benefactors in our lives, regarding their aid to us as something they morally ought to provide. Here too God, if he exists, should be functioning as a benefactor of last resort. Yet clearly that has not generally been happening.

Swinburne wants to argue that God while sharing the same morality with us is not subject to the same requirements to prevent rather than permit especially horrendous natural evil consequences from being inflicted on us when such prevention is needed. However, the arguments that Swinburne uses in the context of natural evil parallel the arguments that he used in the context of moral evil. Given that I have shown that these earlier arguments did not work, Swinburne's arguments with regard to moral evil are not going to work with regard to natural evil either.

g. Compensation

The role for compensation in Swinburne's defence of God's permission of especially horrendous evil consequences of immoral actions requires that God's permission of those consequences be morally justified as the logically necessary means for securing the important freedom of the would-be perpetrators to impose those consequences on others. Now I have shown that the freedom of would-be perpetrators of horrendous evil consequences cannot serve as a moral justification for God's permitting those consequences for the following reasons because:

(1) It comes at the cost of significant freedoms.
(2) Its beneficiaries would morally prefer not to have it, given the equal freedom they would otherwise have and given that they are required to prevent its especially horrendous consequences themselves.
(3) We cannot altogether enjoy this same freedom, and
(4) Exercising this freedom works against achieving the highest virtue (in part by severely restricting the significant freedom of its victims).

My argument, therefore, precludes any justification for God's compensating those who have suffered from horrendous evil consequences because the all-good God of traditional theism cannot compensate for what he should have prevented in the first place. Only imperfect moral agents, like ourselves, can get into situations where we must do that. A justified role for God's compensating for especially horrendous evil consequences of immoral actions that he should have prevented is not a logical possibility, and so any God who would engage in such compensation rather than preventing horrendous evil from being inflicted on us in the first place would not be the super-benefactor of traditional theism. Accordingly, Swinburne's claim that the God of traditional theism can always remain a benefactor for someone whose life on earth is on balance bad by giving them a good life after death is actually necessarily false.[13] The God of traditional theism, if he exists, cannot provide goods that would-be beneficiaries would morally prefer not to have (See my discussion of MEPR II), the provision of which cannot be justified by the freedoms at stake, and then make up for the horrendous evil consequences that logically accompany those goods by providing other goods in an afterlife that could be provided without permitting those horrendous evil consequences.

Nevertheless, it is useful to note how Swinburne thinks compensation is said to work in the Christian story of redemption. In general, there are two kinds of compensation. There is compensation for harm/wrongs caused by justified acts and there is the compensation for harm/wrongs caused by unjustified acts. The Christian story of redemption assumes (we now see mistakenly) that God was morally justified in giving us unlimited freedom to act wrongly if we wish to do so. As Swinburne tells the story, we acted wrongly against God, and this necessitated the need for the second sort of compensation, compensation for the wrongs caused by unjustified acts if our relationship with God was ever to be restored. Notice that the focus here is on restoring our relationship with God, not on restoring our relationship with our fellow creatures whom we also have wronged.

In Swinburne's telling of the Christian story of redemption, proper compensation for wrongdoing directed against God himself is provided by the life and death of the incarnate son of God through whom we are empowered to restore our relationship with God. The compensation that God ensures for himself is the offering of the perfectly good life of his own incarnate son to make up for our initial failure to provide God with the good lives we are said to owe to him. By contrast, we ourselves are compensated, Swinburne tells us, by the assurance that either in this life or in this life extended to include an afterlife, no one would be better off if one had never existed except through one's own choices.

If you think these contrasting outcomes are the result of the application of the same moral principle governing compensation for horrendous wrongdoing, think again. It is the lack of a comparably justifiable compensation scheme with respect to serious wrongdoing against those we are assuming to be fellow creatures that shows that an all-good, all-powerful God of traditional theism, if he exists, had to prevent those consequences rather than permit them. This is just another indication of why the God of traditional theism is logically incompatible with all the evil in our world. Swinburne was able to come up with an initially plausible compensation scheme for wrongdoing directed against God himself, but he was not able to provide a comparable scheme for wrongdoing directed against our fellow creatures. This is because there is no logically possible way for the God of traditional theism to appropriately compensate for horrendous evil consequences he conclusively should have prevented in the first place.

It is worth pointing out here that while the compensation story cannot even get going with respect to ourselves and other victims of the imposition of the horrendous evil consequences of immoral actions given that those consequences should have been prevented rather than permitted, the story could still have been morally justified if it was just God himself who was being wronged. This is because, as I argued in my first essay, the God of traditional theism, if he exists, should not prevent the consequences of wrongful acts that are directed *solely* at himself, given that, as the God of traditional theism, he would be invulnerable to harm from any wrongful acts that were just directed at himself. Hence, God would have had good reason to fully respect our freedom in this regard by not preventing the consequences of wrongful actions that are directed simply at himself, while still maintaining that such wrongdoing requires rectification.

Nevertheless, the justification for God's permission of the evil consequences of wrongful actions still fails even for wrongful deeds that are directly only at God himself because God did not need to permit the suffering and death of Jesus to provide adequate compensation for those wrongful deeds. Just about any hardship suffered by Christ would have sufficed. From a theological perspective, any way that Christ could have lived a good life would have sufficed to bring about our redemption in this regard. Moreover, if God had prevented the horrendous suffering that was said to be imposed on Christ, his life on earth would be more like that of a Nelson Mandela, a Dolores Huerta, or a Mohandas Gandhi (without his assassination), each of whom in different ways provided a powerful example of how we should live our lives. Hence, in theory, if God existed, and the Incarnation occurred, there was a way for such compensation to be morally acceptable, at least in the case of compensation for wrongdoing directed only against God. It is just that it could not have been justified given Swinburne's recounting of the story of Christian redemption.[14]

h. Super-Benefactor

So far in this essay, I have not directly challenged Swinburne's initial assumption that God is our super-benefactor, which is used in

Swinburne's application of GBC I.[15] Rather, I have argued that Swinburne's failure to provide a comparable justification either in terms of greater freedom or greater virtue for God's permission of horrendous evil consequences in the world as is required by his GBC II undercuts any possibility that God is our benefactor or super-benefactor. While this suffices to defeat Swinburne's theodicy, here I want to directly take up that initial assumption of God's being a super-benefactor that Swinburne makes.

So, let us assume that God, if he exists, would have benefited us by causing the Big Bang. Yet after benefiting us in that way, barring miracles, all of the other ways God, if he exists, would be benefiting us would be through the actions of human beings and natural processes. Moreover, given that in the case of moral evils, theists generally assume that it is, not God, but human malefactors who are primarily responsible for the moral evil in the world, so too in the case of moral goods, it should be, not God, but human benefactors who are primarily responsible for the moral goods in the world. Swinburne himself says we should be completely free to do good or evil in the world, and so even on his own account, we should be understood to be primarily responsible for all the moral good and moral evil that thereby occurs in the world. Of course, God, like others, could be thought to sustain us in existence where that is understood as not doing what would cause us to not exist, but that is not a way of benefiting us but rather a way of not harming us. Hence, it would not be a way that God would show himself to be our benefactor.

Now God, if he exists, could show himself to be our benefactor by acting independently of human agents and natural processes to provide us with moral goods. There are countless ways that God could do this and thereby show himself to be our benefactor. It is just that there is no credible evidence that God, if he exists, is systematically and universally providing us with any moral goods in this way. Hence, in the context of moral goods, God, if he exists, would not be showing himself to be a greater benefactor than human agents taken all together have shown themselves to be.

With respect to moral evils, as indicated above, we can agree with theists who generally assume that it is human malefactors who would be primarily responsible for the moral evil that would be in the world. Nevertheless, we can also maintain that the God of traditional theism would be subject, like ourselves, to MEPR I–III. Abiding by these minimal unconditional requirements of morality, as the God of traditional theism, if he exists would do, would both have drastically reduced the amount of moral evil in the world for which human malefactors would still be primarily responsible and clearly establish God as a super-benefactor.

Now earlier in this section of my essay, I have shown, sometimes appealing to Swinburne's own moral standards of freedom and virtue, that given the evil in the world, no such God, who is our benefactor or super-benefactor, could exist. I do not want to repeat that argument here.

Instead, I want to do two things. First, I want to consider the way Swinburne uses the idea of the good of being of use, mentioned earlier, and related ideas to make what would have to be, if God exists, his permission of horrendous evil consequences of immoral action appear morally defensible, and hence, more like the actions that a benefactor would engage in than is the case. Second, I want to briefly take up the question of how Swinburne's idea of a God who is a benefactor/super-benefactor relates to the evolutionary history of life on our planet.

So here is the most problematic case where Swinburne employs the idea of the good of being of use:

> [Consider] the case of babies abused by their parents, who die before they can get any pleasure out of life at all. It is still the case that their life is of great value, because by their openness to such abuse, they provided their parents with the choice either of abusing them or not abusing them; and so by their availability to suffering, they made available a great good for the parents, which alas the parents misused. Also, what has happened to the child normally becomes known and so leads to measures in the community to avoid such abuse in future.

Thus, on Swinburne's analysis, the free choice of parents whether to abuse their babies was a 'great good' for their parents and the use their babies endured was a good as well, a good of use. But on my analysis, the freedom the parents exercised was a freedom that they should not have exercised whereas the freedom of their babies not to have the horrendous abuse inflicted on them was a freedom that their babies surely should have been able to enjoy. Moreover, the God of traditional theism could never adequately compensate in an afterlife for his failure to prevent such horrendous evil consequences that he easily could have, and should have, prevented in this life. Likewise, morally good people could never be intimate friends with a God who wrongfully failed to come to their aid when that aid was most needed, conclusively required, and could easily have been provided (see MEPR II).

Consequently, the parents' choice was not a great good but rather a great evil that should have been prevented. Likewise, while the babies were used by their abusive parents, there is virtually nothing good about that use. It is just another way of characterizing the evil that occurred in these circumstances and should have been prevented. It is not morally good for babies to be of use to their abusers. In such cases, the victims would morally prefer not to have horrendous suffering imposed on them, and the perpetrators, if they ever repented their deeds, would always morally prefer that they had been prevented from imposing those consequences on their victims by God as a last resort.

Let us turn then to consider how well Swinburne's idea of a benefactor/super-benefactor God relates to the evolutionary history of life on our planet. Let us allow that the God of traditional theism caused the Big Bang and thereby what has transpired thereafter. Then let's ask whether what we know about what has transpired since the Big Bang is compatible with the God of tradition theism, if he exists, being a benefactor of living beings generally, and of human beings, in particular.

In this regard, it has to be disconcerting how long it took before life at all, and human life in particular, appeared in our universe. Cosmologists tell us that the Big Bang occurred 13.7 billion years ago but that life on earth only appeared 3.5 billion years ago and our own species, Homo sapiens, appeared only 300,000 years ago. Moreover, if all the time it took before life in general and human life in particular came into existence is not troubling enough, worse still is that when life finally did appear on earth, it went through five mass extinctions over a period of 500 million years before human life finally managed to emerge. And even then, human life only made the scene because a large meteor just happened to strike the earth causing a climatic disaster that drove the dinosaurs to extinction, thereby giving mammals the chance to evolve and spread over earth, leading eventually to the emergence of our own species. Finally, to note just one last unfriendly feature of the universe we inhabit, cosmologists tell us that the universe, as we know it, is destined to eventually end in a heat death where there will be no life, no planets, no stars, just a universe that is ever expanding, nearly empty, cold, and dark.

Of course, we already know what an origin story for the universe that depicts the God of traditional theism as a benefactor would look like. It is dramatically recounted in the scriptures of the Judaeo-Christian-Islamic religious tradition. However, the scientific story of the origin and subsequent history of the universe, even when God is assumed to be the cause of the Big Bang and thereby what comes thereafter, has a quite different look to it from what we would reasonably expect from the all-good, all-powerful God of traditional theism, even if we did not have an argument now derivable from Swinburne's moral requirements as well as my own, that such a God is logically incompatible with all the evil in the world.

i. Examples

Here I will discuss several examples Swinburne mentioned over the course of his essay and indicate how they should be understood in the light of my argument.

(1) Swinburne asks us to consider someone badly injured and left severely disabled for life by a railroad accident which in turn led to the development of a new system of railway signalling that would prevent similar accidents in the future. Surely, Swinburne asks us to conclude, this further consequence of the accident is better than if it served no useful purpose at all. While this is surely the case, it would have been even better if, as required most likely by my NEPR I or II, God had intervened to prevent most, but not all, of the person's injury in such a way that it was still discernible to those who investigated the accident what went wrong with the train system and what needs to be fixed to prevent such accidents in the future. Of course, if this accident was due to negligence or

poor design, then MEPR I or II would apply to it rather than NEPR I or II.

(2) Swinburne considers a number of ways that political states could reduce rape and child abuse and argues that they would produce more harm than good if political states were to use them. He then suggests that the same would hold true for God. Unfortunately, Swinburne does not take into account how God could prevent the horrendous consequences of brutal assaults and child abuse without the overreach, misfires, and abuse that could characterize badly designed, institutional attempts. All that God has to do is intervene just before the horrendous evil consequences of wrongdoings are coming down on their victims to avoid the infliction of those evil consequences on them, as needed. That is just what would-be victims would morally expect the political states to which they belong to do with the morally acceptable means that are at their disposal. Here too God's intervention could suggest ways that we ourselves could better detect and prevent horrendously evil consequences so that eventually virtually all the prevention that was needed could be accomplished without God's intervention.

(3) As for Covid-19, who would complain if God had intervened just when the virus was about to inflict especially its horrendous evil consequences on its victims, and to do so in such a way that researchers would be able to figure out how to neutralize the virus in the future themselves? Who would complain about God intervening in this way—surely not the millions who have died or are likely to die from the virus in the world? Of course, some people, as we have seen in the current Covid-19 epidemic, want to be free to impose unnecessary seriously harmful risks on themselves and others. Even so, morally good people operating through political states, as well as the God of traditional theism, if he exists, would have sufficiently good reasons to restrain these advocates of unrestrained freedom.

(4) Near the end of his essay, Swinburne tells us about a SS soldier who was content to obey orders to treat people of occupied Poland in various cruel ways until he was commanded to set light to a house into which many Jews had been crowded. He obeyed the command;

but, as he heard the screams of the burning Jews, he did not suppress his horror at what he was doing and was moved to a deep genuine repentance, and so began a journey on the road to sanctity.

Swinburne reminds us that these choices would not have been open to this SS soldier without the possibility of horrendous evils. Accordingly, Swinburne presents this as an example of a success story for God's permission of horrendous evil in the world.

But I don't regard it as a success story. Suppose the soldier had truly repented and continued to do so in any afterlife. Won't that soldier have then always morally preferred that God had prevented him from inflicting horrendous evil consequences on others, and especially on the Jews he helped herd into a building and burn alive? God then, knowing what would be the soldier's moral preference, would have respected that preference, and so restricted the freedom of the soldier to inflict those consequences on his victims.

Now if God had done this, how would the soldier have responded? One possibility is that soldier, realizing that his ability to inflict evil consequences on others was significantly restricted, would not have repented, but just continued in his evil ways, so restricted, both in this life, and let us assume, in any afterlife as well.[16] The other possibility is that the soldier, no longer able to inflict horrendous evil consequences on others, would repent his evil intentions and the lesser evils he caused, and over time become a morally good person. Either of these possibilities would be a morally acceptable outcome for the God of traditional theism to permit, and neither would have involved God's permission of horrendous evil consequences.

It is also important to recognize that God's providing us with the great good of having the opportunity to be friends with himself cannot be conditional on God's permission of horrendous evil consequences of immoral actions. If it were, we would not be dealing with the all-powerful God of traditional theism. The same holds true for God's providing us with resources necessary for a decent life. Hence, God could have prevented the horrendous evil consequences of the SS soldier's actions without depriving anyone of the opportunity to be friends with himself or of the resources necessary for a decent life.

Notice too how much better it would be for those who would otherwise be the victims of horrendous evil consequences, like those inflicted by the SS soldier, to live in a world where God prevented such consequences, as needed. While they would still experience some adversity, they would all have the same significant freedom to live their lives, and they would all be morally better off on that account.

Lastly, Swinburne's example of the SS soldier is based on a central figure in Simon Wiesenthal's personal narrative in *The Sunflower*. In the narrative, an SS soldier, who is dying in a hospital, requests to see a Jew. Wiesenthal, a forced labourer working nearby, is brought to him. The solder then confesses to Wiesenthal his life history culminating in the horrific killing of Jews in which he participated and for which he now begs for forgiveness. From this account, it is clear this SS soldier would have morally preferred that God, described as 'on leave' in the narrative, had intervened to prevent him from inflicting horrendous evil consequences on his victims. The SS soldier would not have regarded himself as a success case for God's permitting of horrendous evil in the world.

j. A Misinterpretation, a Clarification, and Some Objections

Here I have collected together a misinterpretation that I would like to clear up, a clarification I would like to make, and a few objections that still needs answering.

A Misinterpretation

The most important misinterpretation that Swinburne makes of my view occurs in the following passage. Swinburne writes:

> And in writing 'creatures that exist in this world are almost all, as far as we can tell, better off existing than not existing'. Sterba would seem to admit that – if God exists – he does ensure just that for almost all of us. (Chapter 3 p. 38)

This misinterpretation would not have occurred if Swinburne had just continued his last sentence with 'and yet, he thinks, God is required to do far more'. Without that additional clause, however, Swinburne makes it appear that we both are endorsing his GBC I as a way of capturing the morality that the God of traditional theism would be required to uphold after creation. Yet my proposal for capturing the morality that would apply to God after creation is given by the much more demanding MEPR I–III. That is why Swinburne tried in his essay to undercut these requirements with counterexamples. So, Swinburne should not be suggesting, as he does in the quoted passage and the surrounding text, that we both endorse his GBC I as a standard of ethics for God after creation.

A Clarification

Swinburne claims on Chapter 3, p. 39 that the onus is on me to show that there is no afterlife, and he claims on Chapter 3, p. 49, note 7 that the onus is also on me to show that we do not have a free will. But my argument that the God of traditional theism is incompatible with all the evil in the world works even when, for the sake of argument, I have granted theists the assumption that there is a heavenly afterlife. In fact, part of my argument builds on that very assumption. In addition, as I made clear in *Is A Good God Logically Possible?* I have also assumed, for the sake of argument, a libertarian understanding of free will.[17]

Two Objections

Objection 1

Now when I argued that the gross disparities of freedom that exist in our world between those inflicting horrendous evil consequences and their victims are morally unjustified and should not have been permitted in the first place, Swinburne countered that 'God, like a good parent, gives different assignments [of freedom] to different children' (Chapter 3, p. 55). Here, and elsewhere, Swinburne attempts to analogize differences of radical injustice to differences that are not even differences of injustice at all. Surely, some differences in freedoms are defensible in family relations but those differences can never be used to justify, even by analogy, permitting, for example, the radical difference in freedom that obtained during the Holocaust between the Nazi perpetrators of horrendous evil consequences and their Jewish victims, especially those victims whose gas chamber fate was anything but chosen.

But what about the beneficiaries of God's permission of horrendous evils, like the Holocaust? Given that the would-be beneficiaries of the consequences of God's permitting horrendous evils, like the Holocaust, could have (1) the greatest good of the opportunity to be friends with God, (2) the resources for a decent life, (3) an equal opportunity for soul-making, as well as (4) many other goods that God could provide them, all without God's permitting any horrendous evil consequences, the would-be beneficiaries would conclusively morally prefer that God have prevented rather than permitted those consequences because of all the above goods they can receive that are independent of such consequences and because the goods that are so depended on those consequences are goods they don't otherwise need and can easily do without. In addition, the would-be beneficiaries of God's permission of horrendous evils, like the Holocaust, would also morally prefer not to be implicated in the violation of people's fundamental rights on which such goods depend, especially given that the would-be beneficiaries don't otherwise need and can easily do without them.

Moreover, the victims of horrendous evils, like the Holocaust, cannot be adequately compensated by the goods that are logically connected to those evil consequences that are inflicted on them because those goods are only goods they don't really need and can easily do without. Other goods, worth having, like the opportunity to be friends with God, the resources for a decent life, an equal opportunity for soul-making, and other such goods are all goods that God could provide to us without permitting horrendous evil consequences to be inflicted on us, and as such they cannot serve as an adequate compensation for the infliction of such horrendous consequences on us. Thus, you cannot compensate someone for horrendous harm done to them by giving them would you should have or would have given them even if no such harm had been inflicted on them. Horrendous evil consequences, like those of the Holocaust, are not evils that the all-good, all-powerful God of traditional theism could have dealt with by permission followed by adequate compensation. The God of traditional theism would have been required to just prevent and not permit such consequences. Permission of such evil consequences, like those of the Holocaust, followed by adequate compensation was never a moral possibility for the God of traditional theism, as my MEPR I–III attest. It would also make those who would be compensated significantly worse off than they would or should have been.

Knowing all this, perpetrators of horrendous evil consequences on innocent victims, if they ever morally repented their deeds, would always wish they had been stopped before they were about to inflict those consequences on their victim by the God of traditional theism if needed, as last resort.

Objection 2

At one point, Swinburne suggests that the difference between the two of us is simply a quantitative one concerning the amount of suffering an all-good, all-powerful God of traditional theism would be justified in permitting. Now it is true that Swinburne and I both agree that God, if he exists, would be justified in permitting non-horrendous evils in the world for the sake of soul-making. However, with respect to horrendous evil consequences, our views are starkly different. Swinburne argues that the God of traditional theism is morally justified in permitting all such consequences that occur in the world while I have argued that he would not be morally justified in permitting any of them. Consequently, it would be a mistake to describe our difference here as being simply a quantitative one concerning how much evil God, if he exists, could justifiably permit. Rather, the difference is primarily a qualitative one where I argue that God cannot consistently permit any horrendous evil consequences but only non-horrendous ones such as significant or trivial evil ones, paradigm cases of which we have no problem recognizing in real life. By contrast, Swinburne seemingly acknowledges these qualitative differences between evils, but then argues that God is still justified in permitting them all. Hence, the difference between Swinburne and myself is really over the justification for all the horrendous evil consequences in the world—a qualitatively distinguishable evil. Swinburne argues that God is justified in permitting all such evil consequences and I argue that God is justified in permitting none of them. Our debate then is over the presence of a certain kind of evil, not the presence of a certain amount of evil. Given that my argument works then for a multitude of paradigm cases of horrendous evil, there is no need to be able to clearly distinguish every case of horrendous evil consequences from every case of non-horrendous evil consequences.

Moreover, it would be a mistake to think of the difference between horrendous evil and non-horrendous evil, and more specifically significant evil, as simply a quantitative one with horrendous evils simply involving more suffering than significant or other non-horrendous evils. (Think of Bentham's analogous claim for goods that 'push-pin is as good as poetry.') This is because many horrendous evils, like the Holocaust, the slave trade, and what has been called the American Holocaust (which by 1890 had resulted in a 98 per cent decline of the native population of North America from pre-Columbian times) have a structural component to them that qualitatively distinguishes them from other evils.[18]

Now Swinburne recognizes that evils, particularly significant and horrendous ones, are logically related to certain goods that they make possible. For example, the occurrence of a rape is logically related to securing the opportunity to console a rape victim. Thus, significant and horrendous evil are qualitatively distinguished from each other, at least in part, by the different goods they make logically possible. But this contradicts Swinburne's further claim that what constitutes a 'horrendous' evil, rather than merely a 'significant' evil is a quantitative matter. If significant and horrendous evils are qualitatively distinguished by the particular goods their permission makes logically possible then they are not constituted simply by how much evil they make possible.

It is also the case that many, if not most, horrendous evils that have occurred over the course of human history, like those mentioned above, typically have a structural component to them. This structural component involves correlated action and inaction of many different socially positioned individuals operating within a shared wrongful perspective of what ought to be done or permitted with some individuals being more responsible than others for the evil that results. This structural component is frequently lacking for significant evils, as it is by the natural evil of being struck by lightning and by the moral evil of being struck by a reckless driver. Hence, it is clearly not the case that what distinguishes a horrendous evil from a merely significant one is a quantitative matter.

V. A Conclusion and More

In the first section of this essay, I set out a version of my argument that the God of traditional theism is logically incompatible with all the evil in the world. In the second section, I reply to the two counterexamples that Swinburne raises against the necessary normative premises of that argument, primarily MEPR II. In the third and longest section of the essay, I deal in detail with Swinburne's own argument for the compatibility of the God of traditional theism with all the evil in the world and conclude that given Swinburne's own normative premises, the God of traditional theism is logically incompatible with all the evil in the world.

To begin, there are two explicit moral premises to Swinburne's argument which are GBC I–II. Nevertheless, these two moral premises do not fully capture Swinburne's normative view because they do not directly mention the goals of freedom and virtue which are central to the moral stance that Swinburne claims is used by God. So let me express Swinburne's normative view this way:

(1) God is justified in permitting all the evil in the world for the sake of the freedom it makes possible.
(2) God is justified in permitting all the freedom in the world for the sake of the virtuous results it makes possible.

Now the discussion we had in (a) of how best to support freedom requires us to revise (1) to:

(1*) God is justified in permitting all the evil in the world for the sake of the freedom it makes possible, but not permitting horrendous evil consequences of immoral actions because God's helping us to prevent those consequences, as needed, would result in greater significant freedom overall.

Similarly, the discussion we had in (e) of how best to be virtuous requires us to revise (2) to:

(2*) God is justified in permitting all the freedom in the world for the virtue it makes possible, but not in permitting the freedom to inflict horrendous evil consequences on others because, like a just political state, God's helping us to prevent those freedoms, as needed, would result in greater virtue.

In light of (1*) and (2*), if the God of traditional theism exists, then to promote significant freedom and greater virtue, as he would be required to do, God would have to prevent all the horrendous evil consequences in the world, as needed. Clearly, that has not happened. Hence, given the moral premises of Swinburne's argument, as I have explicated them, the God of traditional theism is logically incompatible with all the evil in the world.

Of course, Swinburne may not want to interpret his moral premises in the way I have just done. My only response is that my interpretation emphasizes the importance of both significant freedom and greater virtue which are fundamental to morality, as well as to Swinburne's own view, and so it should be acceptable to interpret Swinburne's normative premises in the way I have just done.

Still, although the moral premises of Swinburne's argument, as captured by (1*) and (2*), are logically incompatible with all the evil in the world, they still fail to constitute a logical argument from evil because we can entertain the possibility that there are exceptions to (1*) and (2*) that would serve a greater good. Fortunately, no comparable objection applies to my argument.[19] Hence, it remains a logical argument from evil against the existence of the God of traditional theism.

a) How I Got Here

In our Introduction, Swinburne and I explained how Alvin Plantinga was able to defeat John Mackie's argument that the God of traditional theism was logically incompatible with all the evil in the world. Basically, what Plantinga did was reject the two premises that Mackie put forth as necessary premises which when joined with the assumptions of the argument from evil that God and evil exists were supposed to yield a contradiction. That would have shown that the God of traditional theism was logically incompatible with all the evil in the world. Instead, it was fairly easy for Plantinga to show that the two premises that Mackie offered up were not even true, let alone necessarily true.

As it turned out, Plantinga's overturning of Mackie's argument was a pivotal event in the contemporary discussion of the problem of evil. After Mackie lost his debate with Plantinga, it was not clear how anyone inclined to defend atheism could continue to approach the problem of evil as Mackie had done. This helps explain why philosophers who still wanted to defend atheism turned their attention to a new strategy—that of developing what came to be called evidential arguments for atheism. All this meant was that atheists were no longer trying, as Mackie had, to add necessary premises to their arguments in support of atheism. A consensus had formed that 'logical' formulations of the problem of evil were untenable. Thus, most atheists after Mackie's failed attempt at a logical argument from evil have simply tried to argue that the God of traditional theism is improbable. Hence, the uniqueness of my argument that the God of traditional theism is logically incompatible with all the evil in the world.

That I was able to come up with this argument is due, in large part, to my being an outsider to the way that work on the problem of evil has been done by philosophers who worked on the topic since the failure of Mackie's argument. If during the years following the Plantinga/Mackie exchange, while the consensus that Mackie-style logical arguments from evil were untenable held sway, I had been working in philosophy of religion, I would most surely never have come up with the argument I now have. It was only because I was able to draw on my work in moral and political philosophy, and eventually come up with exceptionless, minimal components of the Pauline Principle that are necessary requirements of morality as well as employ categories from political philosophy that enabled me to consider all the goods with which God could provide us that I was able to produce the Mackie-style argument I have been defending in this book.

5
Response to Sterba's Response

Richard Swinburne

I. Sterba's Main Detailed Objections to My Theodicy

In the first part of this second essay, I will respond to what I take to be James Sterba's main detailed objections to my theodicy. In the second part I will briefly summarize my main argument, applying it especially to some of the world's worst evils. In the final part I will respond to Sterba's 'evolutionary argument'. I shall not discuss Sterba's criticism (ch4, 95–96) of my account of the Christian doctrine of how the life and death of Christ provided redemption for human sins, since my answer to the question which our two essays consider, does not in any way depend on that account.

I begin by responding to Sterba's objection to the relevance to his MEPR II of my two examples where parents have the right to permit others to impose some evil on their children. Sterba objected that since the evils concerned are only 'significant evils', and his MEPR II is a principle forbidding the imposition of 'horrendous evils', these examples have no relevance. But I was not putting forward my examples as direct counterexamples to Sterba's MEPR II. What I wrote (ch3, 46) was 'If parents whose responsibility for the existence, nurture, and security of their children is very limited, have very limited rights of the kind described, it becomes highly plausible to suppose that God whose responsibility for the existence of humans lasts as long as they exist[1] and is so much greater than that of a parent, has the right to impose much greater evil on humans for the sake of the moral well-being of the sufferer and of other humans.' If parents have the right to impose evils of a certain kind on their children for the sake of a limited moral good (at most, one making it more likely that their earthly life would be fairly morally good), then a being who had far more responsibility for the existence of those children and far more understanding of what would be the effect of the evils on those children and others, will have the right to impose far greater evils on those children for the sake of a far greater good (their freely chosen sanctity). The responsibility of God as the ultimate cause of all the good things humans enjoy, giving most of them an overall good life on earth, and God's ability to give all humans abundant good in an afterlife, enables him to fulfil my GBC I very easily. We get our understanding of what it would be for an omnipotent and omniscient creator to be morally good, from our understanding of what it is for a parent of only little power and little understanding, and little responsibility for the existence of their children, to be morally good. Good parents would allow their children to suffer a certain amount if it makes possible the significant good of them choosing freely to live a good earthly life. A perfectly good creator would allow the rational creatures whom he creates to suffer quite a lot, if it makes possible the enormous good of them choosing freely to live the very best everlasting life.

Of course if 'horrendous evils' were evils of totally different kind from 'significant evils', then Sterba's objection to the relevance of these examples would be appropriate. But, I claimed, 'horrendous evils' are just worse evils than 'significant evils'; the difference is just a difference of degree. One criterion for an evil to be 'horrendous' rather than merely 'significant' might be that, like the Holocaust, the slave trade, or the Gulag it is an evil suffered by a large number of humans. But a choice may be just as evil if it caused in just one human being suffering similar to that caused in many human beings by such paradigmatic horrendous moral evils. How evil a choice is, is largely a matter of how much suffering of what kind for how long an agent is prepared to impose on another person. I would call it a 'horrendous' evil if just one African was captured and taken into slavery, shackled, forced to row across the Atlantic for many weeks, and thereafter forced to work on a plantation for many hours a day for many years, whether or not this happened to many other Africans. But whether you call an evil 'horrendous' not merely if it is the foreseen result of a choice to cause great suffering of a certain kind for a certain length of time, but also if it causes it to a large number of people, all of these factors are matters of degree. To judge by Sterba's own example of the kidnapped boy—it would only have been a significant evil, if such an African was captured, enslaved for a few days, and forced to row someone for many miles upriver. The differences are certainly very large, but they are quantitative differences. Sterba claims (ch4, 107) that evils such as 'the Holocaust, the slave trade, and what is being called the American Holocaust... have an institutional structural component to them that qualitatively distinguishes them from other evils'. But that institutional component consists in an evil done to each of the victims, that they are being deprived of their cultural inheritance; it's not an evil done to some super-entity, the society; and so again it is a matter of how many people suffer and how great is the deprivation, which are matters of degree.

Sterba misunderstands my claim that 'the difference between "significant" and "horrendous" evils is a matter of degree' (ch3, 59) or a 'quantitative' rather than 'qualitative' one. Of course—see (ch4, 106–107)—different evils (whether horrendous or merely significant) are often logically related to different goods which they make possible; some evils make one good possible, and other evils make a different good possible. But I can't see why it is supposed to follow from that, that horrendous evils are qualitatively (as opposed to quantitatively) different from non-horrendous evils. Sterba follows his claim 'that many, if not most, horrendous evils typically have a structural component to them' by claiming that 'the structural component involves correlated action and inaction of many different socially positioned individuals operating within a shared wrongful perspective of what ought to be done or permitted.' But surely the only evils involved in an evil such as the slave trade, which has such a 'structured' character, are the evils suffered by the individual slaves, and the evils perpetrated by slave ship captains and slave ship owners and condoned by many citizens. Of course the evils perpetrated by slave ship owners are worse than the evil perpetrated by the owner of a single slave; but that is because the slave ship owner knowingly causes far more suffering, than does the owner of a single slave. But again, that is a quantitative matter. Sterba seems to have a picture of an evil committed by some society, which is additional to any evil committed by any of its members. But I think that is a wrong picture, because societies don't have 'intentions' or 'beliefs' in literal senses. The 'intentions' and 'beliefs' of a society are analysable in terms of the intentions and beliefs of many of its members. For that reason, I suggest that what constitutes a 'horrendous' evil, rather than merely a 'significant' evil is a quantitative matter, for example of the degree of suffering caused to how many people and the length of time for which it is caused. I shall in future use as my criterion for a 'horrendous' evil, that it is the foreseen result of a choice that causes great suffering to one or more sufferers.

Given that understanding of 'horrendous evil actions', Sterba argues that if some of us do such actions, the consequences of such actions will 'preclude others from having the same freedom that the perpetrators exercised' (ch4, 88). However, I was not arguing that the world would be better if everyone had a kind of freedom which I described, only that it would not be worse. So if some humans have different ranges of freedom from those which other humans have, that is not a good argument against the existence of God. I claimed (ch3, 62) that 'God, like a good parent, gives different assignments to different children'. Sterba argues (ch4, 76) that the 'would-be beneficiaries of the consequences of God permitting horrendous evils' could have 'the greatest good of the opportunity to be friends with God, the resources for a different life [and] an equal opportunity for soul-making ... as well as many other goods, with or without God is permitting any horrendous evil consequences'. He claims that these are such radical differences of freedom, that those who suffer horrendous evils are being treated totally unjustly in comparison with others, including those who perpetrate the horrendous evils. But he has not taken my point that God is concerned, not merely we should have a 'decent life', but that we should have the life of saints and that if we deal with horrendous evils correctly, we shall become saints by our own free choice. And, as I argued (ch2, 62), only saints would be happy living the life of heaven everlastingly. That is the sort of 'soul-making', not Sterba's low-grade soul-making, which we need for our ultimate wellbeing. Many of us have the opportunity to do very good actions of courageously bearing and helping others courageously to bear the natural evils of disease, accident, and the weakness of old age, as well as moral evils inflicted on us by others. But doing such ordinary very good acts may still leave us with selfish desires to which we are tempted to yield. Then coping in the best way with horrendous evils—for example, by allowing oneself to be killed by a painful process in order to save the lives of others—will surely finally make us saints. To be allowed to suffer for a good cause has been recognized in many cultures as a privilege; and it is surely a great good for us that we have the opportunity to suffer for a very good cause, and thereby to make ourselves saints by our own free choice. And being available to suffer such evils does not merely provide the sufferer with a great choice of how to deal with them, but it provides the perpetrators with the good of a final choice of their own destiny. But it is clearly good, as seems to be the case, that (apart from psychopaths who have little free will) only those who have almost destroyed their sense of morality by freely doing worse and worse evil actions will ever have the opportunity to perpetrate a most evil action which finally destroys that sense. (If some psychopaths are born evil, then of course they are not culpable for their actions; and God might give them in an afterlife that good moral sense of which they were deprived on earth.) Most of us avoid having that opportunity by doing a few good acts.

The point that the evil suffered by different humans differs quantitatively, but not qualitatively, is also relevant to my claim that God has an obligation to ensure that the evil suffered by any one human is outweighed in the course of the whole human's life by the good enjoyed by that human—which was my first normative condition to which even God is subject. It follows from this condition, that if there are humans whose earthly life is such that the good is outweighed by the evil, then God has an obligation to provide for those humans an afterlife in which the evil of their earthly life is outweighed by the overall good of their life before and after death. That will clearly always be possible if all evils not outweighed by good states on earth are only quantitatively different from evils which are outweighed by good. God can just provide after their death more of the good things for any humans whose earthly life is on balance bad.

(Like many other writers) Sterba sometimes makes the mistake of attempting to show that God would never be justified in allowing some evil to occur, by pointing out correctly that human parents or the State would never be justified in allowing that evil to occur. But he pays no attention to my crucial point that since God is so much more our benefactor than they are, it is to be expected that he has the right to allow certain evils to occur—as long as my two conditions are satisfied, when it would not be right for parents or the State to allow those evils. For example, in (ch4, 85) he writes that 'just as we morally expect an ideally just and powerful political State to prevent, where possible, the final stage of especially horrendous evil actions, so likewise, should we morally expect the all-good, all-powerful God of traditional theism' to do the same. He rightly points out here and in (ch4, 86) and again in (ch4, 87) that a just State is not concerned with any of our bad thoughts and intentions which are never likely to have bad effects on others. That is so, because its status as a limited benefactor is limited to ensuring that we fulfil the condition implicit in its benefaction to us that we will obey its laws concerning our public behaviour. But God, as a far greater benefactor who gives us life in order that we should live a very good life, must be concerned with the purity of thoughts involved in living a very good life. In (ch4, 92) Sterba argues largely correctly (but in my view subject to possible qualification—see my example of the bullied son) that parents ought to intervene to stop their children being assaulted, even if doing so would prevent their children from understanding the intrinsic wrongness of immoral actions.[2] Parents have this obligation because, as to a limited degree a source of the existence of their children, they have an obligation to protect their own children from physical harm, and so children have the corresponding right to be protected by their parents. But God, as so much more the cause of the existence and development of all humans, has a far greater right than parents have sometimes to permit children to suffer great harm, for the sake of the much greater good for which he created them and others.

Sterba does however recognize, when claiming (ch2, 73)—correctly—that an ideal political State should ensure that no citizen could impose serious evil on any other citizen, that I will claim that, unlike a State, God, as our supreme benefactor, does have the right to impose very serious evils on us, in order to give us the opportunity to make great differences to ourselves and others, and thereby become saints by our own free choice. He then goes on to argue that if political States were successful in ensuring that no citizen could impose serious evil on any other citizen, then no one would have the opportunity to impose horrendous evils on others, and so 'no one would have the opportunity to be a saint'. I think it most unlikely that political States would ever achieve that goal, except by limiting the freedoms of citizens in ways of kinds which I discussed in (ch3, 56) that we would hold that an ideal State should not impose. But even if an ideal State were to ensure that no citizen could impose serious evil on any other citizen, there would still be plenty of opportunity for us to make ourselves saints, provided by the natural evils of disease, earthquakes, etc. for the victims of such natural evils to cope with the evils in ways which would give them the opportunity to begin to make themselves saints; and for those who choose to do nothing to help the victims, to begin to lose their moral sense. If—implausibly—scientists of the future were able to prevent the onset of all diseases and other natural evils, and to ensure that everyone died only from painless natural causes at the end of a long life, then in that future there would be no problem of evil. But that does not count against my argument, since I am arguing only that a world of our kind is not worse than a world without serious moral and other natural evils; I am not arguing that it is better than such a world.

Sterba suggests that God 'should take a different stance toward the earlier stages of free actions than he takes to the final stage of free actions where horrendous evil consequences are inflicted on their victims by their perpetrators' (ch4, 85; see also ch4, 87); he should allow the perpetrators to decide to inflict a horrendous evil, but then intervene to stop the evil occurring. But if God always did that, would-be perpetrators of horrendous evils would know that it was beyond their power to perpetrate a horrendous evil and so they wouldn't even try. Maybe God could eliminate all our memories of failed attempts to produce horrendous evils, so that we did not realize that it was beyond our power to produce such evils. But that would be highly deceptive of God. A perfectly good God would give us real choices, not put us in a simulator which we do not realize to be a simulator.

However, it might not worry Sterba if God deceived us, since he holds (ch4, 85) that such earlier stages, while 'of moral significance', are of far less importance than the final stage because it would infringe the freedom of victims 'not to have the horrendous evil consequences of immoral actions inflicted on them'. Sterba holds that human well-being consists primarily in what happens to us, and so morality is valuable primarily for the same reason as the laws of States are valuable: that if people act morally, other people will have good things happen to them. I suggest, however, that what we freely choose to do, especially when our free choices produce their intended effects, is more important than what happens to us; that, contrary to Sterba, 'freedom to' is more important than 'freedom from' (although of course that too is important). It is very valuable for humans that they are free to make important differences for good or ill to themselves, other humans, and the world. It is that ability which makes us mini-creators, sharers with God (through God's choice) of bringing about the kind of humans and the kind of world that there are. And it is enormously valuable if we make good choices which make other humans and the world better.[3] And not merely does how we affect other humans and the world matter greatly in itself, but it also matters greatly because by our choices we make ourselves naturally good or naturally bad persons. We would expect God to want to give us freedom of a greater degree but of the same kind as good parents would want to give their own children; they would not want to give their children a drug which will automatically turns them into the sort of children they rightly want them to be.

Sterba's emphasis on the (positive or negative) value of the (good or bad) consequences of our actions as a measure of their worth, leads him to the view that 'constraining one's own freedom ... is what is required to be more virtuous' (ch4, 89). But surely any individual, wealthy or not, will only be 'virtuous' insofar as they do the actions which they justifiably believe will have the best consequences, whether or not those actions do actually have the best consequences; and (ch4, 75) insofar as it is difficult for them to do such actions. Sterba rightly claims that sometimes 'willingly' paying one's taxes to the State to meet the needs of others is more effective than trying to meet those needs oneself; and that leads him to claim that it is sometimes an exercise of greater virtue to abandon one's freedom of choice of what to do with one's money. But if paying taxes is compulsory, one has no freedom to abandon; and if paying taxes is optional, then one is not abandoning one's freedom but continually exercising it in a good way—which is virtuous.

Sterba claims (ch4, 110) that he was able to discover his 'unique' argument 'that the God of traditional theism is logically incompatible with all the evil in the world' because, unlike (in his view) most other philosophers of religion, when he came to write about the philosophy of religion, he was able to draw on work in moral and political philosophy. I suggest that Sterba's work on political philosophy has proved a hindrance and not a help, to his study of philosophy of religion. Political philosophy is concerned with the rights which the State ought to guarantee for its citizens, but Sterba provides no reason to suppose that these rights are the same as the rights which God ought to guarantee for rational creatures; and I have been providing reasons to suppose that they are not at all the same.

Sterba has, however, one intuition about what God might be expected to do, which has no source in political philosophy. This is that the greatest good that God could provide us with is friendship with himself (ch4, 75). Hence, Sterba's argument seems to go, it would be 'morally wrong' for us not to prefer to do without any goods (such as the ability freely either to make ourselves saints or lose our sense of moral goodness), which depend on God permitting the horrible events which would be necessary for us to exercise that choice. We don't need these goods, Sterba claims, if we can enjoy 'the opportunity to be friends with God' (ch4, 77). A God would be able to give us his friendship, Sterba claims, without giving us any large degree of free will. But what does Sterba mean by a human having 'friendship with God'? Friendship with a baby or a dog is different from friendship with another adult; and likewise, we should expect friendship with God to be different from friendship with another adult. We have friendship with someone if we know to some extent who they are, interact with them, listen with some appreciation to what they have to say to us about the world and themselves; we tell them what we think about the world and ourselves; if they ask us to help them or we see that they need help, we provide that help if we can easily do so. We can't be a friend with someone whom we 'meet on the net' and have no idea who they are. So to be a friend with God, we must understand that he is necessarily omnipotent and omniscient—that's what he is; he may well tell us how we should live, and so listening to him with some appreciation will inevitably cause in us the belief that we ought to live in the way he tells us; and so to the extent that we don't do what he says, we are not taking the relationship seriously. All religions teach that to some extent God does seek to interact with many of us in these ways—'God spoke to our ancestors in many various ways by the prophets' (Letter to the Hebrews 1:1); and they teach that some of us listen, and some of us don't. God will want to help us to live in the best way possible, and that— if my arguments are correct—will involve freely choosing to do good acts involving reacting to suffering and overcoming bad desires, which will make differences for good to others and the world and make ourselves saints. So, if God does offer us his friendship, taking up the offer will involve doing just those actions which Sterba claims will not be necessary if God offers us his friendship.! Jesus said, 'You are my friends if you do what I command you' (John 15:14); and the author of the Gospel which reported this saying clearly believed that Jesus is God.

There is anyway no guarantee that God will offer to every human being his friendship during their earthly life. To be in touch with God and to know clearly how we ought to live, and to know that if we do live in that way, God will take us to heaven after death, does make it much easier to do saintly acts. Just as a good parent wants their child to succeed without depending too much on parental help, so too a good God might want humans to succeed without providing too much help; and so he may keep his presence hidden from many humans in order to enable them to do saintly acts just because they are very good to do without the encouragement of a subsequent reward. Surely a good God in the end will make himself known to his rational creatures capable of understanding who he is, but he may judge that it is better for some of us to keep himself in the background for a while. I conclude that whether or not God 'offers us his friendship', we need the goods of being able freely to choose to do good or bad acts which will make great differences to our characters; and that involves the possible occurrence of moral evils and actual occurrence of natural evils.

In sustaining natural processes, God provides for us many more good things than he is obliged to do by my good benefactor conditions (GBC I and II). Without human assistance, sun, rain, and rivers often produce food and drink; and humans can and do use natural processes to make ever more sophisticated good things—bronze and iron, paper and books, electricity and television, and so on and so on. As Sterba acknowledges, God (if he exists) benefits us by sustaining these natural processes. Yet he complains (ch4, 97). God should be showing 'himself to be our benefactor by acting independently of human agents and natural processes' and that would be providing us with 'moral goods'. But just as when we do a morally good action by freely giving someone a present, so God does a morally good action all the time as he keeps natural processes in operation to provide us with the good things of life. Sterba seems to want him also to be continually operating independently of natural processes in order to produce good things. But a good God, like a good parent, would want us to use the tools he has given us to make the world and ourselves as we choose (while of course hoping that we will make the good choices). If he was continually intervening into the operation of natural processes, we would never have the ultimate responsibility for what happens—and having that is his great gift to us. (This is consistent with him intervening occasionally and unpredictably in response to human prayers and needs.)

I sought to make it initially plausible that God would be justified in allowing the occurrence of many horrendous evils affecting many humans, by pointing out that States could prevent the occurrence of evils which are 'nearly horrendous'—the evil of cruelty by many parents to their children, and the evil of prevalent rape—by taking certain strong preventative measures; but that liberal minded citizens normally think that that would be wrong because it would eliminate the possibility of certain greater goods. Liberal minded citizens think that there are greater (not merely comparable) goods which would be eliminated if the State took sufficiently stringent measures to prevent rape and cruelty to children—the good of privacy in our personal lives, and the good of biological parents (however imperfect) bringing up their own children. The point which I was seeking to make by these examples was (ch3, 56) that 'the evils are not so abhorrent that no one would ever be justified in allowing them to occur'. If the evils are not of that immensely evil kind, then God could allow them to occur for the sake of a comparable good, and provide adequate compensation for those who suffer. But Sterba misunderstood the point of the examples when he wrote (ch4, 101) 'Swinburne does not take into account how God could prevent the horrendous consequences of rapes and child abuse without the overreach, misfires, and abuse that could characterize purely human-directed attempts'. The point of the examples was not to show that God could not eliminate these evils in some way other than ways open to the State (and I explicitly acknowledged that he could), but to show that even liberal minded people allow that these evils are not so evil as to outweigh any possible good. I then proceeded to make the further point that the goods made possible by allowing humans freely to choose how to bring up their own children (and, I should add, other humans having the choice of stopping them if they abuse their choice frequently and obviously), and freely to choose whether or not to control their strong sexual and other desires, and in these ways form their own characters (and those of their children) are great goods. And evidently God could not provide these great goods without allowing the possibility of the great evils of child abuse and rape. Hence, I argue that my second moral requirement is satisfied for 'nearly horrendous evils'. (To repeat a point, I certainly think that society ought to try hard to encourage good parenting and respect for of sexual integrity—but society encouraging is not the same as God compelling.) Despite the great good for the parents of being allowed that choice, the earthly lives of babies who die as a result of such abusive treatment were, as I wrote, 'clearly not on balance such that it was good that they had lived them'; and hence, I claimed, God would inevitably compensate them for that abuse, which—though quantitatively great— could always be outweighed by a very good life far longer than the evil of their present life. In my view, no one, not even God, can foresee the result of free choices; but God took the risk of trusting the parents and allowed the evil of the abuse to happen for the sake of the comparable good that the parents could freely make the good choice of caring well for their babies. (My view that not even God can foreknow the result of a free choice seems to be shared by the authors of the book of Genesis (6:6), when they wrote that when God saw the wickedness of humans before the Flood, he was 'sorry that he had made humankind on the earth'.)

Sterba claims (ch4, 88) that the perpetrators of horrendous evils themselves 'if they ever morally repented their wrongful deeds, would for all eternity morally prefer that their freedom had been restricted by God's prevention of the horrendous evil consequences of their actions'. It is certainly true that if someone was truly penitent for having perpetrated a horrendous moral evil, they would for all eternity morally prefer that they had not made the wrong choice—for the victims' sakes, as well as for their own sake. But that's not the same as morally preferring that God had prevented them from having any choice. If they became truly penitent, then their choice would not have been a total disaster—it would have provided them with the opportunity for taking the upward path back to goodness, which they would not have had if God had prevented them from having any choice at all; and even though they would regret greatly that they had abused God's trust and perpetrated the horrendous evil, they might still be grateful that God had trusted them, and given them that opportunity. And Sterba's related claim (ch4, 88) that 'even those who would have acted virtuously...would for also for all eternity morally prefer that their freedom...had been similarly restricted' seems implausible. They would surely be grateful for God having trusted them to prevent the occurrence of a horrendous evil, and be very glad they had done the right thing. (See earlier in this essay for my response to Sterba's claim (ch4, 88) that 'they would only be content if an equal freedom to do good and evil were effectively secured for all'.)

In order to make a choice of how to benefit or harm others or ourselves, we need to know the effects of different actions. And so it is good that scientists among us should study the causes of lung cancer and floods and droughts, financed by taxes which we others pay. But that, I pointed out, requires the actual occurrence of lung cancer, floods, and droughts. Sterba seems to suggest (ch4, 93–94) that once scientists have found the answers, 'much of that knowledge can be passed on to us from others, and they themselves may have acquired it from still others'. But it is always open to question whether the generalizations reached by earlier scientists continue to work in a new situation; there are always new diseases and new weapons of war, and frequently our twenty-first-century sources of information disagree—large numbers of posts on the web tell us that burning fossil fuels is not causing climate warming, while others of course tell us that it is. So, not merely do scientists need to check on the results of earlier science, but we non-scientists need to decide between conflicting sources of scientific information, and that means at least investigating the qualifications of our informants. Sterba suggests that really God ought to be providing all this information for us, or at least allow one group of scientists to find the answers, and then leave us to act on them and get on with our lives. However, I argued, God has given us the great gift of reason, and so it is good that we shall be able to use that gift to find out how the world works, or at least which informants about it prove most reliable, rather than God just giving us the answers.

II. My Main Argument Applied to the World's Worst Evils

The first consideration (my GBC I) determining whether God has the right to permit the moral and natural evils which occur in this world, is whether, despite these evils, God provides each of us with a life which is on balance a good life. I argued in my previous essay that having a good human life would include having much ordinary happiness in a family life and leisure occupations, and most importantly, freely helping others (our family, and others beyond our family) also to have much ordinary happiness and themselves to help others in very significant ways which involve helping ourselves and others to have a certain kind of character. And, given that there is a God, it must include proper interaction with him, involving reverence of him as our perfectly good creator, that is worshipping him, as well as being friends with him. (And, I need to add, God would not be selfish in wanting us to worship him. It is a good thing to reverence what is good; and human parents rightly want their children to reverence them—not for the parents' sake, but for the children's sake.) A God who created us would want us to do all these things, but while it might not be bad if he programmed us to do them, it would be good if he gave us the great gift of a (libertarian) free choice of whether or not to do them. I argued that most humans on earth have that sort of life, and that the moral and natural evils which occur help us to have it; but for those whose life on earth is on balance bad, (I should add) through causes other than their own evil free choices, God would have an obligation to provide a compensatory afterlife. Horrendous evils involve suffering which lasts only a relatively short time (in the scale of eternity), and so, if necessary, can always be compensated by providing the sufferer with a very good life after death, and God would have an obligation to provide this.

The second consideration (my GBC II) determining whether God has the right to permit the moral and natural evils which occur in this world, is whether God permitting these evils makes possible a comparable good which couldn't be achieved in any other morally permissible way. Every natural or moral horrendous evil provides an opportunity for the sufferers to make a great difference to others and themselves by the way in which they react to it—whether with courage, and a willingness to understand and forgive persecutors; or with self-pity and deep hatred. When there is famine in some country (caused by war or natural disaster) many people have the choice of sharing their little food with others in order to keep the others alive; and at all times many more people have the choice of abandoning ambitious projects in order to care for a sick relative. These are greatly good choices which can put us some distance along the way to sanctity, but bad desires may still continue to influence us. We can only reach sanctity by our own free choices of good actions by totally rejecting all self-centred desires, and horrendous evils give us that opportunity to become saints who no longer need to struggle against temptation, since doing good becomes totally natural. These truly unself-centred actions which improve our character are actions of benefiting others for their sake, not actions of benefiting others in order to improve our own character. That the former do improve our character is a knowable good by-product of the former. The Christian religion, and no doubt other religions also, have seen as their greatest glory the saints who have endured much suffering rather than deny their deepest convictions; and States have always given their greatest honours to those who have resisted torture rather than betray their comrades. A God who did not ever give any humans choices of the former kind would be a God who did not trust any humans to make an all-important difference to others and themselves.

Although God would not have an obligation to provide an afterlife for most of us, being perfectly good, he would also want all of us to live a life of being supremely happy and worshipping God and helping others to worship God and helping others in lesser ways, free from temptation to do otherwise, and free from pain—for ever in heaven. It would, however, be good for us to be able to choose freely whether to have such a better life. Being happy living such a life involves enjoying worshipping God and helping others. For most of us on earth some of our happiness consists in having more of the good things of life than other humans have—more power and more prestige; and for some of us alas it consists in seeing other humans suffer. And many of us get only limited enjoyment out of reverencing those who are better humans than we are, let alone reverencing our good creator. Ordinary fairly good humans of these kinds would not enjoy the life of heaven—for ever; we would lust for unavailable lesser pleasures, and be bored by singing the praises of God. Only the saints would be totally happy in heaven; and although perhaps God may make some people saints without their having chosen to be thus, I suggest that it is good that people should freely choose whether or not to be saints. So it is good, not merely for our own sake on earth, but for our life after death, that God gives us many choices, including a final choice of coping with a horrendous evil, whereby by choosing rightly we can, gradually or not so gradually, make ourselves saints.

Also, since each time we do a bad act of some kind, it becomes more natural to do a bad act of that kind next time, God gives us the opportunity gradually to become worse and worse people. Just as it is good that it should be up to us whether or not we become saints, it is also good that in the end it is up to us whether we become unchangeably bad people. Choosing to let just one child starve to death, or to kill someone by dousing them in oil and setting light to it, are surely greatly evil acts that can make us lose much of our moral sense. But doing more and more significant evil acts of stealing, breaking up a marriage, or ignoring the starving can also put us some distance along the way to losing our moral sense. Clearly a good God is not going to let us become unchangeably bad people without providing us with many opportunities to make a good choice and reverse the downward trend, and much encouragement to do so. Because of an unhappy and morally bad upbringing, some find it initially a lot harder than others to make good choices; they begin the process of character formation from a lower platform. Hence God would need to provide for these unfortunates even more opportunities than for others. And maybe some of us who have not made ourselves totally saintly or totally evil, have choices after death by which we can complete the process of making ourselves saints, or lose any sense of morality—see (ch3, 63).

But in the end anyone who is not even penitent at having done a greatly evil act would finally 'lose their soul'. If we suppose that God would always ensure that every human becomes a good human, that would deprive all our choices of a considerable part of their significance. And if we could always go on for ever making choices of a kind which affect our character, we might never finally be able to make ourselves a certain kind of person, and that too would deprive all our choices of a considerable part of their significance. So while having the choice of whether or not to do a greatly evil act or even just to be penitent for having done so, gives someone the opportunity to begin to take the route back to goodness, it also gives them the opportunity finally to lose their moral sense. Since to see an action as morally good entails having some (however weak) inclination to do it, such a being who ceases to be influenced by moral considerations would no longer recognize actions as 'morally good' or 'morally bad', but merely as 'what others call "morally good" or what others call "morally bad"'; and so in an important respect would cease to be a human being. It is good that humans should have the ultimate choice of the sort of person they are to be. But there is no other way in which this can be achieved despite the nagging of their consciences ,except by this continued suppression of conscience involved in doing really horrendous acts; and that is a further reason why God permits horrendous moral evils. There are different afterlife fates God might provide for such beings who have annihilated their consciences. He might condemn them to sensory pains in hell, or simply eliminate them, or (as in George Bernard Shaw's vision of Hell in *Man and Superman*) give them a life where they would follow trivial pursuits for ever. But they would all, through their own choice, suffer 'damnation', in its original sense of 'loss' of God.

Even the horrendous evils which some humans perpetrate and other humans suffer, are limited in time and intensity—the finite time of a human life before a natural death, and an intensity which is not so intense as to cause premature death. Any period of suffering by one human on earth is very short indeed on the scale of that everlasting life which God could give to humans, and which—according to most theistic religions—will give to many of us. And it is the possibility of these evils which allows the sufferers to make an ultimate free commitment which makes them saints; and the perpetrators to allow themselves to 'lose their souls'.

III. Sterba's Argument from Evolutionary History

Sterba claims (ch4, 99) that my argument that God is our supreme benefactor does not fit well with the fact that although our universe began 13.7 billion years ago, humans appeared only 300,000 years ago. This might perhaps be puzzling if the only good thing God did was to cause us. But the development of the world of fundamental particles into chemical elements, and their compounds coming together to form galaxies, stars, and planets, smashing into each other and creating new galaxies, and so on, is a marvellous work of art. It is like the kind of fireworks display with which big world sporting events now begin, but of course on an enormously greater scale. Even if God was the only person who could see this great event, it would still be a great good thing; but we humans are now learning to see much of this development through telescopes which reveal the world as it was billions of years ago, and humans have always been able to watch the final stage of this development simply by looking at the night sky. Likewise, the formation and development of life on earth and its evolution by means of natural selection is a beautifully engineered, elegant process. One day, some brilliant human engineer will produce robots which eliminate less successful robots and use spare parts from them to make new and better robots; and this will be hailed as a great scientific achievement. God set such a process in operation on a worldwide scale a few billion years ago, and we can now admire its operation. I cannot see that the occurrence of 'five mass extinctions' of species was a bad thing—is it not good that there were once these species, and now there are different species? And even if 'human life only made the scene because a large meteor just happened to strike the earth', on a theistic view either this was a natural process due to the operation of laws of nature on the original matter of the universe, itself ultimately due to

God; or God intervened in natural processes to bring this about. Either way theism can explain human evolution.

There is, however, one significant problem raised by the evolutionary story, on which Sterba does not comment and so I need to comment, and that is the fact of animal suffering long before the existence of humans. For since the major part of my theodicy depends on the assumption that suffering is caused by humans who have libertarian free will, or enables them to exercise that free will better, and since it is a reasonable assumption that animals do not have libertarian free will, that defence is not available to explain why God would allow animals to suffer. The only ground for believing that some non-human creatures suffer is that when they are stimulated in some way (for example, a pin is stuck into their arm), this causes an event in their brains which is similar to the event caused in our brains by a similar stimulation and causes suffering in us. It is not enough evidence of creatures suffering if when they are stimulated in such a way, they react publicly in the same way as we do (for example, by quickly withdrawing the arm and crying out). It is plausible to suppose that robots made of steel and silicon chips could react to the sort of stimuli which cause us to suffer in the same way as we react, without suffering at all.

Since only vertebrates have brains in any way like our brains, there is no adequate reason to suppose that any creatures other than vertebrates suffer. (Hence, in my view, the irrelevance of the example of 'misery' in Darwin's letter quoted in our Introduction.) It is generally agreed that there are in humans two different neural pathways by which bodily damage affects the brain—the 'discriminative' path which leads to brain events causing us to learn where and of what kind is the damage, and the 'affective' path which leads to brain events causing the suffering. The brain events which are the direct cause of the suffering seem to be ones in a region of the prefrontal cortex called the 'anterior cingulate cortex' (ACC). Since only mammals have an ACC, it cannot be very probable that animals other than mammals suffer. But the prefrontal cortex of humans and other primates differs significantly in various ways from the prefrontal cortex of other mammals, so that it is only recently that it has been recognized that there is a part of the brains of other mammals anatomically similar to the prefrontal cortex of humans, and so worthy of the name of 'prefrontal cortex'. The human prefrontal cortex is three times larger than that of a humanoid primate (such as that of our nearest relative, the chimpanzee), an increase of size which occurred only during the past two million years, which must make a corresponding difference to all its powers.[4] My tentative conclusion from all this, is that fairly probably many mammals suffer, and that fairly probably the ones closest us suffer more than others but fairly probably significantly less than we do; and, although new neuroscientific work may increase or decrease the various probabilities, since animals cannot tell us about their feelings, we are not likely to learn very much more in future.

Animals who are conscious enough to have sensations, may plausibly be supposed to have to some degree also conscious intentions, beliefs, and affections (for their own group, and especially for their own offspring). Hence very often when they suffer pain (of a degree significantly less than ours), they to some degree consciously remember the circumstances in which they suffered and learn to avoid those circumstances; they realize to some degree that other animals of their group who exhibit certain behaviour in response to certain stimuli have certain painful feelings, and so learn to avoid the circumstances which produce these stimuli and to deter others, and especially their offspring, from being in such circumstances; they acquire true beliefs about the geography of their surroundings and about their likely predators, and intentionally at least try to avoid (and often succeed in avoiding) such predators, and intentionally struggle to avoid injury and death, and so on. So although they cannot freely choose one course of action rather than another, their suffering causes them intentionally (unfreely) to do some of these actions of response to their suffering, or the suffering of others of their group. Doing these intentional actions gives meaning and purpose to animal lives. (The most spectacular example of animals learning from the suffering of others is when mother animals act as decoys to keep predators away from their offspring.)[5] They could not do these good intentional actions of response to suffering, unless there was that limited suffering; and those actions, although not nearly as good as good free actions, are good in being of use to themselves and others. (See my ch3, 53) I see no reason to believe that non-sentient animals have any rights, but clearly to my mind sentient animals do have rights. The main such right is the right not to be caused to suffer, but it is clearly a G-right. God, as their creator who sustains them in existence, has the right to curtail that right and so (directly or indirectly via other animals) to cause (or to permit humans freely to cause) animals to suffer if thereby he both makes possible a comparable good, and provides on balance for each animal a good life. I suggest that the limited good normally provided by allowing the limited suffering is a comparable good; and that, as with humans, a large majority of all animal lives are on balance good. But, if the earthly life of some animal is not on balance good, God would have an obligation to give that animal another compensatory life of some finite duration either on this earth or on another planet; and that in his omnipotence he could do. As with the similar argument about humans (see ch3, 39), if a large majority of animal lives are on balance good, it is not implausible to explain exceptions to them in the same way that our overall hypothesis (of theism) explains why we cannot directly check that humans have a life after death.[6] So, I conclude that on the evidence currently available, animal suffering is not a strong objection to the existence of God.

IV. Conclusion

In conclusion, I return to our primary concern—human suffering. I suggest that the primary difference between Sterba and myself concerns our view of how a perfectly good God would act towards the humans whom he has created with libertarian free will. Sterba seems to think that God should provide for us a comfortable earthly life of many decades in which we could enjoy many ordinary pleasures, and, if we so chose, make very limited differences to each other and the world. My view is that God would trust us to look after each other and the world, so that it depended to a very large extent for the limited period of an earthly human life on us, whether we and our fellows live good lives and care for each other and the world which he has given us, or bad lives in which we hurt each other and the world; and in the process make ourselves certain sorts of persons. God doesn't want us to be merely fairly good people who would do the right thing if it's not too difficult, but wants us (ideally, freely to choose) to be saints who are totally dedicated to the good. And for that purpose, there needs to be much suffering (as well as much joy) in the world which we could increase or decrease. But he's not going to let the process of each of us being saved or becoming totally immoral go on indefinitely. Either on earth or perhaps after this life, our character must be finally formed: and then there will be no more need for suffering (for the very good, and perhaps also for the totally immoral—unless they so choose).

As I reflect on this argument, it seems to me correct. But I then reflect on just how horrendous is some of the horrendous suffering which God hopes that we will cope with; and so I say to God 'You do expect a lot from humans!' But then I add 'But of course you do—you wouldn't be God if you didn't.'

Notes

Chapter 1

1. See David Hume, *Dialogues Concerning Natural Religion* (Hafner Publishing Co., 1948), p. 66.
2. Letter of 22 May 1860, Darwin Correspondence Project, "Letter no. 2814," accessed on 11 January 2024, https://www.darwinproject.ac.uk/letter/?docId=letters/DCP-LETT-2814.xml.
3. J. L Mackie, 'Evil and Omnipotence', *Mind*, 64 (1955), 200–12, reprinted in many different collections of articles on philosophy of religion.
4. Alvin Plantinga, *God, Freedom, and Evil* (George Allen & Unwin, 1974), pp. 7–64.
5. Mackie endorsed this assumption in his argument with Plantinga even though he himself did not think there is an objective morality.

Chapter 2

1. Given that my goals are much more fundamental than simply raising a feminist critique to traditional theism, I am not going to question here the traditional practice of referring to God simply with masculine pronouns.
2. While I have chosen to put my argument in terms of goods to which we have a right and goods to which we do not have a right, I could have put it in terms of goods that others have an obligation or a duty to provide us with and goods that others do not have an obligation or duty to provide us with. It would have just been more cumbersome to put my argument in this other way.
3. For X to logically presuppose Y here and similarly for X to logically depend on Y means that it is not logically possible for X to obtain without Y also obtaining. See the discussion of logical possibility in the Introduction.
4. Consequentialists maintain that morality is justified simply in terms of the consequences of actions. Nonconsequentialists, although granting the moral relevance of consequences of our actions, maintain that other factors, such their fairness, are also morally relevant. See the chapters on consequentialism and nonconsequentialism in my *What is Ethics?* (Polity Press, 2019).

5. Note that consequentialists can accept the constraint of this minimal component of the Pauline Principle because it has a consequentialist as well as a nonconsequentialist justification. This is a place where their justifications overlap, thus supporting the same requirements.
6. The first of these two possibilities is taken up by MEPR II while the second is taken up by MEPR III. It is important to note here that MEPR I applies to just those cases where the question at issue is simply whether to prevent or permit the infliction of especially horrendous evil consequences of immoral action and nothing more. Once the question at issue is broadened to include consideration of possible goods that might be thought to justify the permission of evils, the question falls under the domains of MEPR II or MEPR III rather than that of MEPR I. Still, all three MEPRs provide exceptionless requirements for their respective domains of application.
7. A moral preference here is a preference that it would be morally wrong not to have.
8. Sometimes I am assuming a conclusive right as here. At other times, as the 'not having a right' in the next sentence, I am assuming just a prima facie right.
9. Soul-making is the activity of developing one's soul or character, virtuously. In these envisioned acts of soul-making, the evil consequences are logically necessary for the good consequences to obtain. Here we might be tempted to follow Marilyn Adams and say that the good and evil consequences form an organic unity, except that the notion of organic unity requires that the good of the whole be greater than the good of its parts evaluated separately. In the soul-making contexts we are considering, however, the good consequences cannot exist without the bad ones. Hence, they cannot be determined to have less value before they are joined with the bad ones. So, the idea of organic unity seems inappropriate to use here. See Marilyn McCord Adams, *Horrendous Evils* (Cornell University Press, 1999), Chapter 2.
10. In response to an objection from William Hasker, I have restricted the application of my MEPRs from 'significant and especially horrendous evil consequences' to just 'especially horrendous evil consequences', as needed, thereby more clearly avoiding a kindergarten objection.
11. For this objection, see John Hicks, *Philosophy of Religion*, 2nd edition (Prentice-Hall, 1973), pp. 40–3 and Richard Swinburne, *Providence and the Problem of Evil* (Clarendon Press, 1998), Chapter 10.
12. The 'as needed' clause is used here to indicate that God should only be the preventer of last resort.
13. Surely if you or I acquired the power of such a state to prevent all murders, serious assaults, etc., as needed, without violating anyone's rights, and we were ideally just, would we not choose to do so? So then would an all-good,

all-powerful God, if he existed, not do the same given that my argument would have ruled out the possibility, at least in God's case, that not doing so would have justifiably prevented a greater evil or secured a greater good?
14. The other non-sentient living beings are other non-sentient living beings who either exist or would definitely exist. Non-human sentient living beings who just could exist, that is, possible non-human sentient beings, have no moral status here. This last condition of this requirement would be violated if God or ourselves attempted to intervene in the conflict between the Ichneumonidae and the caterpillars it preys upon for the purpose of preventing harm to one or the other of them.
15. Anselm, 'Cur Deus Homo', in Thomas Williams (ed.), *Anselm: Basic Writings* (Hackett, 2007), pp. 237–326.
16. Brian Huffling, 'God is Not a Moral Being', *Skeptic Magazine*, 24, no. 4 (2019), 43–5.
17. Ibid., p. 45.
18. Charles Hartshorne, *A Natural Theology for our Time* (Open Court, 1967); Alfred Whitehead, *Religion in the Making* (Macmillan, 1926).

Chapter 3

1. Most substantially in *The Existence of God*, 2nd edition (Oxford University Press, 2004); and more briefly and simply in *Is There a God?*, revised edition (Oxford University Press, 2010).
2. I have argued for this view at full length in *Providence and the Problem of Evil*, and at shorter length in *The Existence of God*, Chapters 10 and 11, *Is There a God?* Chapter 6, and in various articles.
3. On the view that I am expounding, it is not itself a fundamental moral truth that humans have an obligation to obey God's commands, but it is a consequence—on the assumption that God is our creator—of a fundamental moral truth that beneficiaries have an obligation (within limits) to obey the commands of benefactors to use their gifts in particular ways. This latter fundamental moral truth is independent of the will of God.
4. My claim that, if God has commanded certain actions, every human has an obligation to do those actions, is a claim about what is objectively thus whether or not humans believe that. People are only culpable for not doing what they believe to be obligatory, or for doing what they believe to be wrong (= obligatory not to do). So those who honestly believe that there is no God, or who honestly believe that he has not commanded certain actions, are not culpable for not doing those actions.

5. For other positive arguments in favour of the truths of Christian doctrine, including life after death, see my short book *Was Jesus God?* (Oxford University Press, 2008).
6. More precisely, I mean by an agent's action of causing or helping to cause an evil making possible 'a comparable good' that the expected utility of their action is not negative. The expected utility of an action which may cause (or constitute) either an evil state or a good state is {the probability that the action will be one causing (or constituting) the good state multiplied by the goodness of the good state} minus {the probability that action will be one causing (or constituting) the evil state multiplied by the badness of the evil state}. This definition assumes that we can indicate in a very rough way how good is the good state relative to how bad is the evil state by means of arbitrary numbers; and so, for example, if the good state is twice as good as the evil state is bad, we can indicate that by measuring the goodness of the good state as '2', and the badness of the evil state as '1'. The more probable it is (= the nearer to 1 is the probability) that the good state will occur, the more the badness of the bad state may exceed the goodness of the good state, while the expected value remains non-negative. So when God permits a free agent to cause either a good state or a bad state, and the strength of their desires for each state measures the probability that they will cause that state, the stronger the desires influencing the agent to cause the good state, and the weaker the desires influencing them to cause the bad state, the more the badness of the bad state can exceed the goodness of the good state, while the expected value remains non-negative. Since humans cannot give exact numerical values to the relative goodness or badness of states, I use the loose description in the text of an action causing or helping to cause an evil which makes possible a state of 'comparable goodness', to summarize the action having a non—negative expected utility.
7. See my *Mind, Brain, and Free Will* (Oxford University Press, 2013), Chapter 7, for arguments in defence of the view that it is most improbable that science will ever be able to show that we do or do not have libertarian free will, and that on balance the evidence supports the claim that we do have such free will. If it were to turn out that humans do not have such free will, and that our actions are fully determined by our brain states, and these are fully determined by causes outside our control, my main argument for the compatibility of the world's actual evils with the existence of God would fail. But the onus is on Sterba to show that we do not have such free will, if he is to show that for this reason the evils of this world are not compatible with the goodness of God.

8. See my 'Why the Life of Heaven Is Supremely Worth Living', in T. R. Byerly and E. J. Silverman (eds.), *Paradise Understood: New Philosophical Essays about Heaven* (Oxford University Press, 2017), Chapter 17.
9. Alexander Solzhenitsyn, *The Gulag Archipelago*, I–II, trans. T. P. Whitney (Collins and Harvill Press, 1974), p. 175.
10. Simon Wiesenthal, *The Sunflower* (W. H. Allen, 1970), p. 88. Thanks to Eleonore Stump for this reference.

Chapter 4

1. While I have chosen to put my argument in terms of goods to which we have a right and goods to which we do not have a right, I could have put it in terms of goods that others have an obligation or a duty to provide us with and goods that others do not have an obligation or duty to provide us with. It would have just been more cumbersome to put my argument in this other way.

    Now when I included this very same endnote at the beginning of my first essay, Swinburne claimed that it was an acknowledgement that some individual or group A has a moral right only if some other individual or group B has a moral obligation to allow A to do some action, or to provide some good for A. (See Chapter 3, p. 33.) This is correct. Swinburne then went on to claim my discussion in the text seems to assume that if A has a moral right, and B is able easily to satisfy it, then (unless another person C does so) necessarily B has an obligation to do so, which Swinburne claims is false. (See Chapter 3, p. 33) But this is incorrect. What I am further assuming, in light of my MEPRs, is that if A has a moral right, and B is able easily to satisfy it without violating anyone's rights, then necessarily B has an obligation to do so, or at least this is the case when the prevention of horrendous evil consequences is at stake. Thus, to deal with Swinburne's purported counterexample, one would not have an obligation to prevent especially horrendous evil consequences, even if one could easily do so, as long as someone else had a prior obligation to prevent those consequences, and was ready and willing to do so. To claim otherwise, would be a violation of one's rights.
2. This counterargument is frequently ignored by defenders of theism.
3. Sometimes I refer to my MEPRs as exceptionless moral requirements and sometimes I refer to them as necessary moral requirements. For me, they are both exceptionless and necessary, but always calling them exceptionless, necessary moral requirements seemed too cumbersome.
4. Nor to become friends with God would we have to be freer than an ideally just political state would allow.

5. But this could only be the case if moral preference is also understood in a prima facie sense which is not the way I am using it.
6. The exception clause is found in Swinburne's *The Existence of God*, p. 262.
7. A similar mistake is made by political libertarians when they fail to see that the conflict between the rich and the poor is not just a conflict between the liberty of the rich and the needs of the poor, but also can be described as a conflict between the liberty of the rich and the liberty of the poor. For more on this similar mistake, see my *From Rationality to Equality* (Oxford University Press, 2015), pp. 106–7. These two mistakes are quite significant for their respective fields of political philosophy and philosophy of religion.
8. The earlier stages are still morally important for us to have since they provide us with an opportunity for soul-making but without themselves inflicting especially horrendous evil consequences on others.
9. *Providence and the Problem of Evil*, p. 163.
10. To give people this option would require doing things like leaving people completely free to pay or not pay their taxes, supposedly to exercise high virtue. Yet any country with this strategy for collecting taxes would not long last let alone achieve high virtue.
11. If constraining one's freedom to impose horrendous evil consequence on others through the coercive structures of a political state is required for high virtue, then it similarly is required that we constrain our desires to impose such consequences on others. This undermines Swinburne's parallel thesis that high virtue requires that we have strong desires to do great good and great evil. Standardly, a person who reluctantly chooses not to viciously assault someone has not shown high virtue. Nor has a parent who chooses not to torture to death his young child. Choosing not to do a hideous crime is expected of us; it is not the way we display high virtue.
12. *Providence and the Problem of Evil*, Chapter 10.
13. See Swinburne's first essay Chapter 3 p. 58. It is necessarily false because the action described is a conclusively immoral action and the God of traditional theism cannot perform conclusively immoral actions.
14. This is because given Swinburne's recounting of the story of Christian redemption, God's permitting the horrendous suffering and death of Jesus was unnecessary, and hence, unjustified as the means for achieving our redemption.
15. Note that bringing a person into existence may not even be a way of benefiting that person. Benefiting seems to be a process that presupposes a subject that either existed, exists, or will exist independently of that process.
16. For an account of the afterlife that even theists could find acceptable, see my 'Eliminating the Problem of Hell', *Religious Studies*, 56, no. 2 (2018), 181–93.
17. *Is a Good God Logically Possible?* (Palgrave Macmillan, 2019), Chapter 2.

18. See, in particular, David Stannard, *American Holocaust* (Oxford University Press, 1992).
19. Swinburne raises a similar objection to my argument from evil by providing counterexamples to my MEPR II, which I show don't even apply to my argument.

Chapter 5

1. Sterba objects (ch4 note 14, 139) that benefiting a person seems to presuppose that that person already existed, or would exist independently of that process. I would deny that. But, if we allow Sterba's objection, I can make my basic point by claiming that, the moment that person comes into existence, God benefits them by sustaining them in existence for their subsequent life.
2. In her recent book *God, Suffering, and the Value of Free Will* (Oxford University Press, 2021), pp. 50-1, Laura Ekstrom discusses the same example, writing 'if you are a threatening person coming after my children with obvious intent to harm them, your free will would have absolutely zero value in my calculation over what to do'; and she generalizes this to claim that 'we simply do not think that the free will of perpetrators has *value in itself* that ought to figure into our calculations concerning the overall value of a situation'. Her view about what a parent ought to do in such a situation is surely correct, but she neglects the point that a parent's obligation is to protect her own child and so the child's right to be protected by their parent, are different from the obligations of God to that child and equally to all other children and their corresponding rights. (see ch5, 116) I suggest that God would value very much would-be perpetrators of assaults on the weak having the opportunity to recognize the evil of such acts and show pity by not perpetrating the assault. If they do show pity, they will have made one step back towards sanctity. The God of Jesus's parable (Luke 15:3-7) is prepared to leave ninety-nine sheep 'in the wilderness' in order to save one lost sheep.
3. While having free will is a great good because it makes possible the great good of a good free act, obviously to abuse it by doing a wrong action is worse than doing a wrong action when the agent is not free to do anything else. In *God, Suffering, and the Value of Free Will*, p. 51, Laura Ekstrom claims that my view has the opposite counterintuitive consequence: 'If an action's being committed of the agent's own free will brings the intrinsic value of acting with free will into the equation of the overall value or disvalue of the situation involving the harmful act, then a free harmful act will be overall better than a harmful act that does not have added to its disvalue the (alleged intrinsic positive) value of free will.' However, that

consequence would only follow if the 'overall value or disvalue' is the *sum* of two terms—the value of free will, and the value (positive or negative) of a beneficial or harmful act. I suggest, on the contrary, that the positive value of free will is that (while there is great value in simply having free will) exercising it *multiplies greatly* the value (positive or negative) of a beneficial or harmful act, and so the overall disvalue of the harmful act is much greater if it is done with free will than if it is not done with free will. Ekstrom claims (p. 51, n. 33) that in a conversation I agreed that my view had the counterintuitive consequence which she drew from it. I do not remember exactly what I said in that conversation, but if I did say what she attributes to me, I certainly should not have done; and I do not recognize that as a consequence of my view.
4. For some of the scientific details see C. Allen et al., 'Deciphering Animal Pain', in M. Aydede (ed.), *Pain: New Essays on Its Nature and the Methodology of Its Study* (MIT Press, 2005), Chapter 20. There has been considerable neuroscientific study of the functions of different parts of the brain in different animals, subsequent to 2005; but such as I have studied does not seem to alter the general picture very much. But if it were discovered that many more animals suffer a lot more than I suppose, that would constitute a significant objection to the existence of God.
5. For somewhat more detailed exposition of some of the good effects caused by animals suffering by natural causes and the bad intentional actions of other animals, see the pages referred to under 'animals' and 'fawn caught in fire' in the index of my book, *Providence and the Problem of Evil*.
6. Trent Dougherty (*The Problem of Animal Pain* (Palgrave Macmillan, 2014)) seems to defend a theodicy that depends on all animals (not merely some sentient animals whose earthly life has been on balance bad) having an afterlife, and an afterlife in which they have the same cognitive abilities as humans to become saints. I argue that the most that theism might need to postulate is a short afterlife for some animals in which they have good experiences which outweigh the bad experiences of their earthly life. Christian tradition (unlike Eastern religions) has normally assumed that no animals have an afterlife. Dougherty claims (his pp. 158–62), relying on the fuller discussion in Deborah M. Jones, *The School of Compassion: A Roman Catholic Theology of Animals* (Gracewing, 2009) to find some support for his view in Christian tradition; but the only one of the examples of theologians or biblical passages that support it which he provides which seem to share in full his very wide view is that of John Wesley. It is less distant from mainstream Christian tradition, and more in line with two other examples which Dougherty quotes, to hold that animals are resurrected as animals and not with human capacities.

Guide to Further Reading

There is an enormous philosophical literature about the topic of this book, and there are several further approaches to it, which readers might like to follow up, but which we did not discuss in this book, because neither of us was sympathetic to them.

One such approach, favoured by more theists than any other approach, is sceptical theism, which claims that God is so much more knowledgeable than we are, that humans are not competent to judge whether or not God would be justified in permitting some evil. For a discussion of variants of this view, see:

Michael Bergmann, 'Skeptical Theism and the Problem of Evil', in T. P. Flint and M. Rea (eds.), *The Oxford Handbook of Philosophical Theology* (Oxford University Press, 2009), Chapter 17.

For a particular variant of sceptical theism, Wykstra's CORNEA argument, which has provoked much discussion, see:

D. Howard-Snyder, 'Seeing through CORNEA', *International Journal for Philosophy of Religion*, 32 (1992), 25–49.
S. J. Wykstra, 'Rowe's Noseeum Arguments from Evil', in D. Howard-Snyder (ed.), *The Evidential Argument from Evil* (Indiana University Press, 1996), Chapter 7.

Some theists, and in particular Mark Murphy and Brian Davies, have adopted the view that God being perfectly good does not mean God being perfectly morally good (on our understanding of moral). For arguments for and against this position, see:

Brian Davies, *Thinking about God* (Geoffrey Chapman, 1985), Chapter 8.
Mark C. Murphy, *God's Own Ethics* (Oxford University Press, 2017).
M. C. Murphy, E. J. Wielenberg, K. Irwin, and P. Draper, in a book symposium on Mark Murphy's *God's Own Ethics*, in *Religious Studies*, 53 (2017), 545–84.

Alvin Plantinga and many defenders of theism claim only to have produced a 'defence' of why God might allow suffering. A 'defence' is an argument to show that there is no logical contradiction between the claim that there is a perfectly good God, and the claim that there is suffering, because if the world was a certain way (and we do not know that it is not that way), a perfectly good God would have good reason to allow the suffering. In this book Richard Swinburne claimed to produce, not a 'defence', but a 'theodicy', showing that the suffering is such that it is probable that God in fact had good reason to allow it to occur it; and James Sterba argued that even a 'defence' was not possible in the face of the actual evils of the world. Plantinga's own argument is more complicated than we had space to discuss in this book. So readers (with some slight acquaintance with the semantics of possible worlds) might wish to study it, and the objections to it in:

D. Howard-Snyder, 'The Logical Possibility of Evil: Mackie and Plantinga', in J. McBrayer and D. Howard-Snyder (eds.), *The Blackwell Companion to the Problem of Evil* (Wiley, 2013), Chapter 2.
Alvin Plantinga, *God, Freedom, and Evil* (George Allen & Unwin, 1974), part I.
Alvin Plantinga, *The Nature of Necessity* (Oxford University Press, 1974), Chapter 9.

Eleonore Stump has developed in a very full way just how a defence could be provided for the sufferings of particular individuals in her book *Wandering in Darkness* (Oxford University Press, 2010). She does this by giving interpretations of four biblical stories in which different heroes of faith (Job, Samson, Abraham, and Mary of Bethany) are brought close to God through their sufferings. And Peter van Inwagen in his *The Problem of Evil* (Oxford University Press, 2006) has given a full argument to show that a 'defence' in this sense, is available to the charge that suffering as such shows the non-existence of God; and that that is all that someone needs in order to be justified in believing that there is a God.

There is one new kind of theodicy which has not received the attention it deserves. It derives from Leibniz's claim that we are who we are in virtue of everything that happens to us; and so if some evil that in fact we suffered had not happened to us, we would not exist. Robert Adams does not endorse this implausible view in all its fullness; but he does endorse something like the (contestable) principle endorsed by many contemporary philosophers, that it is (metaphysically) impossible that any human could have been born from an egg and sperm different from the one from which they were actually born. ('Metaphysical' impossibility is something like 'logical' impossibility, that is the impossibility of a proposition which entails a contradiction.) It follows that God could not have made us without causing the suffering involved in all the human interactions which eventually led to our birth. He also claims that if we were given a different life from the one we actually had as a result of some event shortly after our birth, we would have lost the particular people whose interaction with us is so much of what we value in life; and that, for that reason, we would prefer our actual life, even if it contains much suffering. Hence for these two reasons, since God loves the particular humans he has created, he would have good reason not to prevent the suffering involved in their existence. See:

Robert Adams, 'Existence, Self-Interest, and the Problem of Evil', in Robert Adams, *The Virtue of Faith* (Oxford University Press, 1987), Chapter 5.
Vince Vitale, *Non-Identity Theodicy: A Grace-Based Response to the Problem of Evil* (Oxford University Press, 2020).

John Schellenberg's book *Divine Hiddenness and Human Reason* (Cornell University Press, 1993) argued that a good God, like a good father, would make his presence known to all the humans whom he created. But since many humans have, not through their own fault, never experienced the presence of God or seen that there are good reasons for believing that there is a God, that shows that, if there is a God, there is a further evil, for which a theodicy or perhaps only a defence is required, to defend theism against atheism.

For an anthology developing and critiquing various kinds of theodicy and 'defence' see:

J. McBrayer and D. Howard-Snyder (eds.), *The Blackwell Companion to the Problem of Evil* (Wiley, 2013).

Earlier books by Sterba and Swinburne on the topic of the problem of evil:

James Sterba, *Is a Good God Logically Possible?* (Palgrave Macmillan, 2019).
Richard Swinburne, *Providence and the Problem of Evil* (Oxford University Press, 1998).

Index

For the benefit of digital users, indexed terms that span two pages (e.g., 52–53) may, on occasion, appear on only one of those pages.

Acts of the Apostles 54–5
Adams, R. 142
after-life, outweighing earthly evil 115
   see also GBC I, and Heaven
Allen, C. 140 n.4
American Holocaust 107
analogy 103–7
   between horrendous evils and family inequalities 104–6
   of just political state 72–4
   rich/poor analogy 77–8
animal suffering 129–31, 140 nn.5–6
Anselm, St 23

babies 37–8, 58–9, 121–2
being of use, good of 28, 53–6, 98–9
benefactors, rights of 33–8
   see also GBC I and GBC II
Bergmann, M. 141
bullied student, example 45–6, 78–9

character formation 51–2, 126–7
child going hungry, example 44–6, 78–9
choice not universalizable 88
children 48–9, 56–9, 121–2
claims 32
compensation 93–6 see also GBC I
CORNEA argument 141
consequentialism 9–13
counterexamples to Sterba's argument, discussion of 78–9
covid 57–8
culpability 135 n.4

Darwin, C. 1–2
Davies, B. 26–7, 141

death, value of 39, 60 see also life after death
deductive proof 65–6
'defence' of theism 141–2
dependence on others 48–9
desires 41, 48–50
divine command theory 5, see also God, right to command
Dougherty, T. 140 n.6

Ekstrom, L. 139 nn.2, 3
Epicurus 1
ethics after creation 24
evidential argument from evil 27
evil persons, totally 63–4, 126–7
evils, *passim*
   defined 1
   moral, defined 1
   natural, defined 1
   quantitatively, not qualitatively, distinguishable 59–61, 106–7, 112–13
   social, not prevented by state 56–7, 101, 121–2
evolution of universe 128–31
existing, benefit of 138 n.14, 139 n.1

fairness of distribution of goods 54–5
free actions, different stages and kinds 84–8, 117–18
free will, libertarian 41, 49, 139–40 n.3
freedom of the agent 7–8
   different stages of 54–5, 86–8, 117–18
freedom, conflicts of 91

GBC I (first good benefactor condition) 38–9, 41–2, 58, 82–4, 111–12, 120–1, 124–5
GBC II (second good benefactor condition) 39–42, 58, 82, 84, 120–1, 125
God, *passim*
  goodness of 141
  a limited God 29–30
  not a moral agent 24–7
  omniscient 35–6, 121–2
  opportunity to be friends with 11–12, 14, 75–7, 102, 114–15, 119–20, 124–5
  revealing his presence 91–2
  right to command 36
  right to be worshipped 124–5
  subject to norms 27
  super-benefactor 32, 80, 94, 96–100, 116–17
  wrongdoing against God, restrictions on 22–3
goods, fourfold classification of 7–8
  to which we have a right 8, 15–17
    first-order 9, 15
    second-order 10, 15
    general provision of 15–17
  to which we do not have a right 12, 17–18
    first-order 13–15
    second-order 14–15
    general provision of 17–19
good, comparable, defined 40–1
good life on earth for most 38, 54
goods, human, listed 47–59
gulag, Soviet 4–5

Heaven 62–3, 125–6
Hebrews, Letter to 119–20
Hell 127
Holocaust 5, 79, 104–7
Howard – Snyder, D. 141
Huffling, B. 24–7

involuntary actions 53

Jesus 62
John, Gospel of St 62
Jones, D.M. 136 n.6

knowledge of causes 52–3, 92–3, 123–4

Leibniz, G.W. 142
life after death 38–9, 58–9, 65, 115, 124–7
  see also GBC I, *and* Heaven
lifeboat cases 20

Mackie, J. 2–4, 19, 29–30, 81–2, 109–10
martyrs 63
McBrayer, J. 142–3
MEPR I (Moral Evil Prevention Requirement I) 9, 15, 19, 40–3, 68–9, 74–6, 79–80, 82, 85–7, 97–8
MEPR II (Moral Evil Prevention Requirement II) 10, 15, 19–22, 40–1, 43–4, 68–9, 74–5, 79–80, 82, 85–7, 97–8, 111–12
MEPR III (Moral Evil Prevention Requirement III) 12, 15, 19–22, 40–3, 68–9, 74–5, 79–80, 82, 85–7, 97–8
mini-creators 49
moral anti-realism 1
moral kindergarten 16–17, 71–2 *see also* toy world
moral principles, Swinburne's, supporting Sterba's conclusion 108–10
moral sense, opportunity to destroy 113–14, 126–7
moral truths, objective 5, 135 n.3
moral views, fundamental 36
Murphy, M. 141

Natural Evil Prevention Requirements (NEPR I–IX) 21–2, 42, 47
non-cognitivism 5
non-consequentialism 9–13
number of sufferers, irrelevant 59–60

origin of life and human life 99–100, 128–31
outsider status, Sterba's 110

parents 34–5, 48–9, 111–12
Pauline principle 9, 19
Plantinga, A. 4, 19, 81–2, 109–10, 141–2
privacy, good of 56
privileges 32 *see also* rights, fundamental
problem of evil 1–2
Purgatory 65

rape 56–7, 121–2
redemption, Christian account of 94–6
responsibility for others 48–9
right to a decent minimum, a 11–12, 14, 75–6
rights, human, legal 32
rights, human, moral *passim*
  fundamental 32–3
  G-, N-, P-, and S-, defined 43–58
  universal declaration of (UDHR) 32–4

saints 61–2, 114–16, 125–6
sceptical theism 13, 141
Schellenberg, J. 141–2
scientific enquiry, value of 52 *see also* knowledge of causes
sexual desires, value of 57

Shaw, G.B. 127
slave trade 4–5, 107
Solzhenitsyn, A. 64
soul-making 114–15 *see also* character formation
SS soldier, example of 64–5, 101–3
State, defined (distinguished from 'state') 33–4 *passim*
Sterba, J., other books and articles of 137 n.3, 138 nn.15–16, 143
  unique argument of 110, 118–19
Stump, E. 142
superman/Clark Kent 18
Swinburne, R. other books and articles of 31–2, 136 nn.5, 7 137 n.8, 138 nn.9, 12, 140 n.5, 143

taxes 34
theodicy 141–2
toy world 59, 63–4 *see also* moral kindergarten
torture 60–2

virtuous choices, more and less 89–92, 118
Vitale, V. 142

Wesley, J. 140 n.6
Wiesenthal, S. 64–5
Wykstra, S. 141